Dreaming the Future

How Our Dreams Prove Psychic Ability Is Real, And Why It Matters

Bruce Siegel

Published by MetaStory Books.
12959 Short Avenue, Los Angeles, CA 90066.

Email: Bruce@BruceSiegel.com
Phone: 310-827-1375

ISBN: 978-0-692-85527-0

CONTENTS

(Dreams are in italics.)

Acknowledgements   v

Introduction   1

PART 1: THE EXPERIMENT   **5**

1. A Door Opens   7
2. Proving the Impossible   9
3. The Figure That Changes Everything   12
4. Method and Definitions   13

PART 2: THE DREAMS   **17**

Using *The Evidence at a Glance* companion   18
5. *The Man Beneath the Spinning Blades*   21
6. Garden Variety Precognitive Dreams: Their Content and M.O.   25
7. *Fallen Limb, Long Odds*   29

PART 3: HOW PRECOGNITION HIDES IN PLAIN SIGHT   **33**

8. The Barriers   35
9. *The Round Object That Merged With a Flat Surface:* A Study in Similarities and Differences   40
10. The Lottery Number Concept   45
11. Metaphors: Revealers/Concealers of The Paranormal   49
12. How Fear Keeps Us In The Dark   52
13. The Ocean in Which We Swim   60

PART 4: SEALING THE DEAL WITH DREAMS THAT COME TRUE IN MINUTES   **65**

14. Two Vast Pools? Answering the Skeptic's Main Objection (*The Student Loan*)   67

15. More on That Shrinking Events Pool   73

16. Lead-Up Dreams: A Punny Thing Happened This Morning As I Was Waking Up   78

17. Two Leadup-Like Dreams (*The Honey-Trap Mystery, Bowling And Reincarnation*)   86

18. A Control Experiment   93

PART 5: MINING YOUR DREAMS   **99**

19. Why These Dreams Matter   101

20. Do *You* Dream The Future?   105

21. How To Observe Precognition On Your Own   109

22. Evaluating The Evidence   117

PART 6: THE LARGER CONTEXT   **123**

23. Awakening to a Greater Reality—My Story   125

24. The Real Subject Here is Consciousness   131

25. Pathfinders, Resources, Further Thoughts   133

26. My Invitation To You   142

APPENDICES   **143**

Appendix A: *The Man Beneath the Spinning Blades*   145

Appendix B: *Fallen Limb, Long Odds*   149

Appendix C: *The Round Object That Merged With A Flat Surface*   151

Appendix D: *The Student Loan*   154

Appendix E: *The Honey-Trap Mystery*   159

Appendix F: *Bowling and Reincarnation*   164

Works Cited   170

To Access *The Evidence at a Glance*   171

About The Author   172

Acknowledgements

I want to thank the following people for helping to make this book a reality:

Leslie Rosenstock, thank you for your insights, your support, and for just plain being my friend. While this may not be the book you would have wished me to write, it's the one I *had* to write—for all of us who have needed to be convinced of a reality that's long been obvious to you.

To Cal Harris, with whom I've discussed these mysteries since way back when my experiment was just getting started: our conversations have helped to make the book possible, and the writing of it, a pleasure.

Joel Steiner and Arthur Steiner (no relation) were especially helpful early readers, and I thank you both.

JoAnn Kailikea—thanks for your kindness, and for irresistible meals served with love.

A special note of appreciation to Leslie Becker, who helps to keep me sane. No small task!

To Christophe Javon: we've drifted apart, but you were my friend for years, and you made a difference.

There's yet more to be said by way of appreciation, but I'm saving that for the next-to-last chapter, where I discuss some of the authors and bloggers who've inspired me.

Introduction

Samuel Taylor Coleridge, the 19th-century poet, asks:

What if you slept
And what if
In your sleep
You dreamed
And what if
In your dream
You went to heaven
And there plucked a strange and beautiful flower
And what if
When you awoke
You had that flower in your hand
Ah, what then?

A haunting scenario for sure. But what is Coleridge really saying? I mean, does anyone believe such a thing could actually happen?

I do.

You see, like Coleridge (assuming he's drawing on personal experience), I have dreams that prove I do the impossible.

No, I may not go to heaven. Nor, on awakening from my dream, do I immediately grasp its importance.

But later in the day, when a vision I've narrated onto my iPhone turns out to have predicted a bizarre, unexpected, event, my sense of wonder surely rivals the poet's.

Because I too end up gazing at a "flower" that *should not be here*: a documented dream that (to give one example) describes in detail an email I received only moments *later*. And what clearer proof could there be of my own inexplicable visit—not to heaven, but to the future?

The phenomenon I'm describing—the experience of seeing the future in a dream or vision—is called precognition. And in these pages, I'll share several encounters with it, along with the corresponding photos and other evidence that turned up only after the dreams were recorded.

If you come to this book as a skeptic: welcome! As a former hard-core materialist/atheist myself, I've spent much of my life walking in your shoes. Even after I began opening up to these things, it took me a long time to fully accept what I was seeing. Much of what I'll have to say is thus written from the perspective of the doubting Thomas I used to be.

But then, skepticism—and its flip side, self-deception—is one of our story's main themes. For the real question is: how did the clues within my dreams escape my notice for so many years?

The answer, it turns out, is compelling. It goes to the heart of what it means to be human. And to appreciate the psychology involved is to begin to wonder if perhaps we're *all* psychic, even if many of us, for reasons of our own, choose to deny it.

But in saying all this, I've yet to mention the true gift here. It's the surprising—and surprisingly friendly—universe such dreams suggest. (Especially in the light of a related phenomenon we'll touch on.)

This more expansive reality is the actual, behind-the-scenes subject of my book, and in later chapters (and in my blog[1]), I address it more directly. For by demonstrating that psychic ability is real, dreams like mine shatter the myth that we are purely physical beings, fixed in time and space within a mechanical universe.

Clearly, we are more.

Which brings us full circle back to Coleridge. For with this poem, he goes beyond sharing his belief in the spiritual dimension, and does something much

---

1   BruceSiegel.net

more powerful: he reminds us of our longing for tangible *proof*, and suggests that it's there for the having.

And this, dear reader, is where precognition, and my book, enter the picture. Since I'm convinced that dreams of the future are common, I devote several chapters to helping you gather your own flowers.

So join me. Grab a basket—or your iPhone—and get ready to encounter the extraordinary.

PART 1: THE EXPERIMENT

1. A Door Opens

If you had known me before my mid-forties you'd understand how ironic it is that I should write a book about dreams that come true. Because for much of my life I would have laughed at the idea that the future can in any way be seen.

To me, psychic phenomena were not, and could not, be real, and I looked down on people who were weak-minded enough to take such things seriously.

This book is about what happened to make me change my mind.

Specifically, it's about an experiment I've been carrying out with my own dreams as the centerpiece, a project that's been going on now for a number of years. Though my professional activities have focused elsewhere, the scientific/spiritual adventure I wish to share with you has been one of the defining experiences of my life.

As to my results, they'll no doubt be hard for some people to believe. Even if you already know the phenomenon is real, you may wonder if I'm exaggerating. So my goal is to show how I proved precognition to *myself*, and then help you follow in my footsteps using your own dreams.

If you're anything like me when it comes to matters of this sort, first-hand experience is the only proof you'll find 100% convincing.

As to why you might want to make the effort, consider this: have you ever suspected there's more to reality than meets the eye? Ever had an unusual experience that made you think the universe is more mysterious—and wonderful—than science is willing or able to acknowledge?

You'd certainly feel that way if you happen to be, by chance, one of the estimated millions of people who've had what's commonly called a near-death experience. The stories surrounding these encounters are by now familiar: the peace, the profound love, the reunion with friends and relatives who've passed, and the resulting certainty that death is not a final ending, but rather a gateway to a separate reality.

Not surprisingly, experiencers often describe their NDE as the single most transformative event in their lives.

What's perhaps less appreciated is how thoroughly researched this phenomenon is by now, and the strength, variety, and sheer abundance of the evidence pointing to the likelihood that what these mystical journeyers report is not mere fantasy.

But if you're on the outside looking in, perhaps you're unimpressed. Maybe you feel that while experiences of this sort may be meaningful for those who've *been* there, what about the rest of us? Why should we take seriously revelations that seem, for all the world, too good to be true?

That's where this book comes in. While its main focus is not spiritually transforming events per se, precognition is, for many of us, such a shocking breach of the familiar, it serves as powerful support for the notion that when near-death experiencers speak of breaking through a veil of illusion, they're neither misguided nor exaggerating.

For if, while our bodies are asleep, we can gain verifiable knowledge of the future (and sometimes of locations we've yet to actually visit), what does that say about the universe we thought we knew? What does it tell us about the limits we've been placing on ourselves? What does it say about what is possible?

Allow me to help you find proof, in your own dreams, that the limitations you've been placing on what's possible may be in error.

If you've been thinking small, this book is an opportunity to change that.

2. Proving the Impossible

Mainstream science says flatly that precognition does not exist. And in such matters we tend to take seriously the opinions of our physicists, mathematicians, psychologists and the like.

Then, of course, there's me, the guy who's telling you those people are wrong. But why should you care what I have to say? All you know about me so far is that I have a strange hobby. And I pursue it largely while asleep.

So I'd like you to know that while I don't buy all of science's assumptions, I like—and have some practice in using—its tools. I'm into logic, numbers, repeatability, and controls.

Most of all, I have a passion for looking at the facts, however odd or unpopular, to see where they lead.

And where many years' worth of facts have led me is this: precognition is real. Such a large percentage of my dreams (and I'll bet yours) point clearly and inexplicably to future events, that insisting coincidence works as an explanation is silly.

How such a momentous truth can remain hidden from so many of us is one of the most compelling parts of the story, and a main theme of this book.

Now I hardly expect the scientific establishment to change its tune because of what I have to say. But that's OK. I'm working with one dreamer at a time here. As I've said, my goal is to help you prove the unbelievable to yourself.

What got me started.

In the early 1990's, for reasons I'll explain later (see Chapter 23), my worldview was shifting dramatically. I found myself becoming interested in certain ideas, experiences, and phenomena I had long dismissed, even ridiculed.

For one thing, I began to pay attention to the fact that some of my dreams seemed to correlate with later events in ways that were difficult to explain. Though on rare occasions I had seen faint hints of this phenomenon before, I had always been certain they were meaningless coincidences, so I didn't give them much thought.

But now, on closer examination, I could see that many of my dreams matched later real-life happenings in multiple and precise ways. The content of these dreams was frequently odd, even bizarre, yet when a dream did come true, it usually happened within hours, or even minutes.

Except for their referencing *upcoming* events, the dreams seemed quite ordinary, so I could see how easy it would have been to forget, ignore, or misinterpret them. As inconceivable as it had once seemed, I was beginning to wonder if, just as we routinely incorporate the *past* into our dreams, we do the same, if unknowingly, with the future.

But despite my newfound openness, I wasn't blind to the laws of probability. I reasoned that given a large number of dreams and the potential for matching them with an even larger pool of waking events, striking similarities were bound to occur from time to time.

After so many years of being absolutely certain that psychic phenomena were illusions created by sloppy and/or wishful thinking, it would take a great deal to convince me that these dreams were truly what they seemed.

What I needed was to see if there were an ongoing, compelling, *pattern* of dreams and correlations. This seemed the only way to know whether or not I was being deceived by random coincidences.

A pioneer in aviation becomes my dream mentor.

During this period I read *An Experiment With Time* by J.W. Dunne. An aeronautical engineer who played a role in the development of powered flight, Dunne, like me, was both surprised and fascinated by experiences he couldn't explain.

In his book, he describes the apparently prophetic dreams that first caught his attention. Fearful for his sanity and determined to understand what was happening, Dunne began to document his dreams in detail, and his methodical approach to studying them provided just the inspiration I needed.

So, following in Dunne's footsteps, I began to record every dream I could remember. As soon as I woke up, I documented each one so there could be no question as to whether I was remembering it accurately.

I soon discovered that many dreams are of little value in a study like this, so I started narrowing my focus to those containing imagery and plot lines that were unusual and unexpected.

As of this writing (2/14/17), I've recorded a total of 241 dreams in an effort to find out what percentage are precognitive. (The project has proceeded in spurts: from 1993 to 1994 I recorded 161 dreams, then stopped, feeling that many of my questions had been answered. In 2010 I picked up the thread once again, and over the next six years recorded an additional 80 dreams. Despite the long lapse, since every dream I document enters into a single pool of data, I think of the whole archive as one experiment.)

As a result, I have indeed uncovered a pattern that leaves little doubt in my mind as to the reality of precognition.

It can be expressed as a simple, surprising, statistic.

3. The Figure That Changes Everything

My experiment shows that roughly one in four of the dreams I document come true, usually within hours.

This is a much more definitive result than I was expecting. It's taken me a long time to trust it. But it's an observation based on many years worth of data, and by now I feel confident in presenting it as fact.

(To be clear, I'm talking about *my* dreams here. While I think it likely that we're all psychic, the percentage of our dreams that relate to the future may vary considerably from person to person.)

Finding such a clear pattern has radically changed how I feel about psychic ability (not to mention the universe itself). Because, stubborn skeptic that I often am, I'm always tempted to look at even my most impressive cases and say: yes, this is weird . . . but still, it *could* be coincidence, right? So many dreams, so many possibilities for finding matches in the real world—this sort of thing is bound to happen now and then.

But I can't think like that anymore. Because now, each time I have a dream that closely parallels a later, real-life event, I have to ask myself: can the law of odds really explain this? Is this the kind, and level, of strangeness that should be showing up in one out of four of my dreams?

4. Method and Definitions

To be clear: the proof of psi (or psychic ability) I offer you, as you read this book, is not contained in my results per se. It consists, rather, of an experiment I encourage you to try on your own. Nearly a hundred years after Dunne's pioneering work, I've taken his approach, expanded on it, and added an original twist or two. But what hasn't changed is the core message: anyone can do it.

I emphasize this now because, having just played up my 1 in 4 success rate, I'd naturally like to be able to prove it to you—but I can't. Because even if you find the dreams presented here compelling, you might wonder if they're representative of my entire database. (They are.) Or you might question my honesty, or find other grounds for skepticism.

So instead, I'll begin by outlining my methods, including how I arrived at that 25% figure, and share in depth a half dozen or so dreams as illustrations.

Then, as promised, I'll present step-by-step instructions to help you get started on your own experiment. If you're anything like me, that—and only that—will satisfy your need to know for certain if the seemingly impossible is real.

Sound like a plan? If so, let's begin by looking at the body of evidence as a whole—how it was gathered and evaluated.

Why I record some dreams and ignore others.

Clearly, the legitimacy of my experiment rests largely on which dreams I include— in other words, which ones I choose to document on waking up. And my rule of thumb is:

I select the dreams that, based on my life circumstances, seem *the least likely to come true.*

Clearly, this speaks volumes about the validity of my results. But what's less obvious is how this approach actually drives *up* my success rate. So let's talk about that.

At first, I recorded every dream without exception. That seemed the only way to discover what percentage might be precognitive.

But it soon became clear that I was wasting time documenting dreams that had no bearing on the matter. And that's because only dreams with content that is specific and out-of-the-ordinary can be proven to be precognitive.

For example, a generic dream about eating breakfast is useless as evidence. After all, I eat breakfast every day. So unless something unusual happens during my dream that is later replicated in my real-life meal, I have no way of knowing if precognition is involved.

Since it's impossible to know if dreams that are routine or vague are psychic or not, eliminating them altogether seems the most sensible approach.

Are you beginning to see how my selection protocol both legitimizes my results, and gives me more successes? The legitimacy aspect should be obvious, and as to my success rate: by not cluttering up my statistics with dreams that haven't even the *potential* to prove psi, I improve the odds that the remaining ones will provide the unequivocal results I'm looking for.

And if you wonder how faithfully I adhere to this guideline, read on. In their strangeness and unpredictability, the cases we'll be looking at speak for themselves, and are representative of my entire database.

(I say a lot more about my procedures in the chapters on how to conduct your own experiment.)

What do I mean when I say a dream "comes true"?

In making claims of precognition, I'm by no means saying that as I sleep, I see something akin to a video recording of what will happen the next day. My dreams are not that accurate or fully fleshed out.

But then, this is exactly what we might expect. For if dreams of the future are real, then it shouldn't surprise us that they mirror upcoming events imperfectly, since that also describes how dreams reflect incidents from the past.

For example, think about dreams you've had that include people you've known or things you've seen. Although such dreams usually contain generous helpings of fantasy, few of us doubt that they refer to actual people, places, things, and experiences.

So when I say my dreams come true, I'm making the same sort of limited claim: regardless of whatever fiction may be mixed in with fact, my dreams contain information—clear and inexplicable *fore*knowledge—about real-life events.

What do I mean by "within hours"?

I probably should have said *usually* within hours because seven of the dreams took from one to five days to come true. However, one of the most compelling features of a large percentage of these cases is their quickness—how little time elapses between dream and matching event. 39% of my dreams came true within an hour, and six of them took less than five *minutes*.

As we go, it will become clear (if it's not already) why the *immediacy* factor makes an already convincing argument for precognition even harder to dismiss.

How I Arrived at 1 in 4.

Each time I wake up from a dream and decide to record it, I'm making a commitment to include it in my statistics. Later, based on the day's events, I'll evaluate it as evidence. (Subject to change on those few occasions when a dream comes true on a later date.)

My scoring system emphasizes these factors: oddness of both dream and event, number and precision of correlations, the likelihood of my knowing about a predicted event through normal means, and how long it took the dream to come true. (I'll describe the evaluation process in detail as we go, and provide a summary with additional guidelines, in the chapter *How to Observe Precognition on Your Own*.)

The possible scores are:

- 0 — Provides no evidence for precognition. (Out of a total of 241 recorded dreams, there are 140 of these.)

- 1 — Suggestive of precognition, but doesn't rise to the level of certainty. (50 dreams.)
- 2 — A solid case. I'd put good money on the dream being genuinely psychic. (51 dreams.)

While I feel certain that many of the 1's (the maybe's) are indeed psychic, to be on the conservative side, I decided to eliminate all of them in determining the percentage of dreams that are precognitive. This should more than compensate for any errors I may have made in scoring the 2's, and it makes the final calculation a simple one: the total number of 2's divided by the total number of dreams (minus the 1's). Or:

51 divided by 191 = .27

If you're concerned about all those 1's I've tossed out, note that even if I labeled them all 0's, the rate of precognition would still be a little more than .21, or 1 in 5. A more accurate approach would probably be to include all the 1's and label half as psychic. That would raise the final figure to .32.

And with that, we're ready to explore the dreams themselves.

PART 2: THE DREAMS

Using *The Evidence at a Glance* companion

Dreaming The Future compares documented dreams to later events with which they share inexplicable common ground. Given our tendency to downplay evidence of "the impossible," it's important that readers be able to grasp all the striking similarities. So for the paperback version, I chose a larger format (7" x 10") that allows the relevant text and images to be displayed on two facing pages.

Ebooks are a different matter, and doing justice to the parallels on small screens has been a challenge. So I've extracted from the book the raw evidence, and condensed it for easy viewing as a PDF document. After printing it (or while viewing it on a separate, larger, screen), you can easily study each dream and matching event while reading ahead in the book's commentary.

Whether you have the paperback or ebook version, this companion is available online for easy downloading, using the password provided on **one of the last pages** of this book.

5. The Man Beneath the Spinning Blades

Having opened the book on a spiritual note, I'd like to say a quick word about the dreams I'm about to share. As you'll see, their content, and the events they foreshadow, are trivial—particularly in contrast to the profoundly moving sorts of experiences that surround near-death, a phenomenon I made such a big

The Man Beneath the Spinning Blades

DREAM (Transcript Excerpts)

Recording completed 8/1/1993 at about 7:20 AM

" I just woke up from a dream with an unusual image in it. It's flying machine that . . consists of kind of like helicopter-type blad There's not really much to this contraption—the blades spinning and you sitting below them."

[NOTE: I meant that last sentence literally—I saw no cabin, blades and a man seated below, completely out in the open. H suspended from the rotors by some crude means that I eithe early, or didn't bother to describe.]

"I just have a strong image of seeing this guy fly down a azed at how close the blades were coming to like telept e[s] . . . I was thinking how can he maneuver this down et without touching occasionally?"

(*The Man Beneath the Spinning Blades, continued*)

MATCHING EVENT

11:30 PM the same day (about 16 hours later)

A news story on workers who repair high-voltage power lines. These are of my TV screen

5. *The Man Beneath the Spinning Blades*

J ust a quick word before we get underway: the dreams we'll be exploring and the events they foreshadow are often trivial. In contrast to the profoundly moving spiritual experiences that surround near-death (a phenomenon I brought to your attention in Chapter One) most of the examples in this book are mundane (not in the sense of ordinary, but earthly).

But then, I'm not excited about these dreams because I find their narratives inspiring. They thrill me, and have indeed changed my life, because by predicting the unpredictable, they've opened my eyes to a universe radically different from the one I thought I knew.

This first example is from 1993, around the time I was just beginning to suspect that many of my dreams are precognitive. As you read, keep reminding yourself: this is the sort of thing that happens with respect to *one out four* dreams I record.

I was watching the 11:00 news one night, and the last segment caught my attention—an offbeat story about a unique approach to maintaining high-voltage power lines.

In this video sequence, we see a helicopter take off from the ground with a man seated *below* the cabin, on the copter's skids. His job is to fly up to the wires, climb onto them, and perform the necessary maintenance.

These are images from the newscast, captured on my VCR.

(helicopter circled)

Video © CBS News Los Angeles 1993

As I watched the story unfold, I remembered a dream I had documented earlier in the day. Here are quotes from my recording for that dream. (The entire transcript for this, as well as each of the other dreams, is in their respective appendices.)

> *"It's 7:10 AM. I just woke up from a dream with an unusual image in it. It's this small flying machine that consists of kind of like helicopter-type blades . . . There's not really much to this contraption—the blades spinning overhead and you sitting below them."*

I meant that last sentence literally—I saw no cabin, just spinning blades and a man seated below, completely out in the open. He was suspended from the rotors by some crude means that I either didn't see clearly, or didn't bother to describe.

"I just have a strong image of seeing this guy fly down a street."

In photos #3 and #4, the power lines on either side give the *impression* he's flying down a street.

"He was just flying about ten feet off the road perhaps . . "

In contrast to typical helicopter flights, this one hugs the ground.

"I was amazed at how close the blades were coming to like telephone poles on the side[s]. . . I was thinking how can he maneuver this down the center of the street without touching occasionally?"

A remarkable match indeed. If a helicopter were flying as just described, it would be hemmed in by power lines precisely as pictured in photo #3.

Weighing the evidence.

The possibility of foreknowledge never comes into play in this case. I had no reason to suspect that anything remotely similar to my dream would later turn up on my TV screen, or anywhere else.

So the crux of the matter is that my dream involves an extraordinary set of circumstances:

- A man is sitting beneath spinning helicopter blades.
- He is seated out in the open, completely exposed to the elements.
- He flies down a street-like corridor,
- precariously threading the narrow passage between power lines that surround him on both sides.

What is the likelihood of dreaming that scenario, and later the same day, encountering it in the real world?

A final thought.

The oddness factor is always high on my list as I weigh the evidence in these cases. And this example is typical in that not only is the event out of the blue, but so is the dream. For while I've dreamt of flight before, never do I remember coming remotely near the situation we've been looking at.

Bottom line: when a once-in-a-lifetime dream is virtually duplicated within hours by an equally rare experience . . . well, here's an analogy that comes to mind: two bullets fired from separate guns colliding in mid-air.

And if you're skeptical, if you're thinking: hey, coincidences do happen, even startling ones; then this is where I remind you that this is not a random anecdote. I'm not just sharing with you an odd experience I had.

With my experiment, I've done what dreamers rarely do—determined how often anomalies of this sort arise in my life. And the fact is, what we've just seen is the sort of strangeness that turns up one out of four times I document a dream.

Coincidence? I don't think so.

(Among other things, the appendix lists four more hits that added to my astonishment while watching the news report, but that, for one reason or another, I didn't document in my original recording.)

6. Garden Variety Precognitive Dreams: Their Content and M.O.

A few points before we turn to another example.

Number one, I'm not writing this book because I think my psychic abilities are especially noteworthy. I know of countless instances of precognition infinitely more impressive than the ones in my archives.

My guess is that we *all* dream about the future, though many of us are unaware of the fact. If my circumstances seem in any way unusual, it's probably only because of how much effort I've put into observing the phenomenon at work.

But my not being a very gifted psychic is right to the point: if the proof within my dreams were too obvious, you might think, "This can't be true for *me*. If evidence for precognition as unmistakable as his were staring me in the face day after day, how could I have missed it all these years?"

And the opposite is equally true. You'd lose interest if my cases were weak or questionable, and maybe feel the urge to remind me that extraordinary claims require extraordinary proof.

Well, the proof we're exploring in this book is indeed extraordinary. Not just because of its strength and frequency (a strength that will become even clearer when we look at dreams that come true in minutes), the evidence is remarkable because of how well it manages to hide.

That is, until we open our eyes, and give it our undivided attention.

All of which is by way of explaining why my garden-variety precognitive dreams (as I like to describe them) are just what we need for understanding how and why psychic ability is both widespread *and* elusive.

As to the content of my dreams . . .

I would have liked to share examples with you that were in themselves insightful or uplifting. But the best proof is often to be found in dreams that, while trivial, are rich in easily identifiable details that are later mirrored in the day's events. In this respect, my more meaningful dreams aren't necessarily what we need.

On the other hand, if the content of these dreams and events is mundane, it's almost always *interesting*. (At least to me, and that's the point.) When my memory of a dream is triggered, it's usually while I'm engrossed in a situation, like watching that helicopter sequence, that would have made me sit up and take notice even without the dream.

Which reminds me: it's no coincidence that the first example I presented involved a newscast. Most of the experiences in the book are, in fact, media-related. TV, books, and the internet are ideal contexts for observing precognition because they provide a wealth of unusual scenarios that the dreamer has no normal way of knowing about beforehand.

Then, too, media events have the advantage of being already documented. Unlike a predicted happening that consists of, let's say, a conversation with a stranger that happens once and then disappears forever, we can re-visit a TV show or blog, and discover additional correlations we may have missed the first time around. Since most of the cases in the book are of this sort, you'll get to see exactly what I saw—the photo or text that grabbed me, and, through the mysterious dynamic we call precognition, made me dream a dream the night *before*.

Making sense of the seemingly impossible.

In re-reading my last sentence, I'm reminded that what I'm saying will sound outrageous to many of my readers. (Believe me, there's a part of *me* that still finds these facts hard to swallow.) So before we go any further, here's how I've come to terms with the logic behind a phenomenon that seems, at first, to make no sense at all.

J.W. Dunne says that precognitive dreams are like ordinary ones except for a single distinguishing characteristic: they reflect the future instead of the past.

I agree. Everything I've experienced over the years leads me to think that whether it's looking forwards in time or backwards, a dream is a dream. Both categories share similar content, as well as the same strange mix of the logical and the fantastic.

Then, too, whether we're immersed in a dream about yesterday or tomorrow, psychologically we find ourselves having roughly the same sort of experience—we *feel* pretty much the same.

So it might be helpful to consider how past-oriented dreams work. Roughly stated, when we dream, we may take pieces or aspects of the "real world"—people, places, events, objects, and so forth—and incorporate them into scenarios of our choosing. The resulting story lines are "true" or "made-up" to varying degrees, but the point is, woven into most dreams are elements drawn from our shared waking reality.

As to why we dream in the first place, the answers are surely as many and varied as the motivations that drive our behavior while awake. All these come to mind: enjoyment, healing, solace, learning, creativity, connecting with others, altruism, and problem-solving.

If we can agree that what I've just said is true for most non-psychic dreams, is it possible that the same applies to *all* dreams, whether of the past or future? If so, we can begin to explore this mystery while standing on somewhat more familiar ground.

How we see into the future.

Likening precognitive dreams to conventional ones sidesteps the central paradox of how we can dream about something before it happens, rather than after. So here are two more propositions to consider.

What if time is a *local* truism, a fact of life in this neck of the woods, but absent from the larger reality of which our physical universe may be only a part?

And what if, while dreaming, we enter that more inclusive realm (or state of consciousness, to be precise), and view events from a vastly different perspective?

If that were the case, then in gathering the raw materials for our dreams, we'd have as much access to future experiences as past ones; we'd be just as likely to incorporate tomorrow's events into our nocturnal dramas as yesterday's.

If what I just said sounds far-fetched to you, considering where I myself start-ed out, I understand. But in looking at my dreams, and I'll bet at yours, you'll continue to run smack-dab into evidence that makes speculations like these un-avoidable.

7. *Fallen Limb, Long Odds*

Here's a dream that predicted the events surrounding a limb falling from my Eugenia tree. Up to then, nothing of the kind had occurred in the *thirty years* I had been living at my current address. While small branches had occasionally dropped from the few trees I've had over that span, nothing larger ever had.

Five days after the dream, though, there was that limb. Its location was as predicted, and my thoughts and feelings on seeing it were just as I had dreamed them.

What happened is that one morning I looked outside and saw that a nine-foot-long, low-lying limb of my Eugenia tree had snapped a foot or two from the trunk. One end was still partially attached to the tree, while the other was resting on the ground, its huge mass of branches and foliage blocking my path and demanding immediate attention.

As I walked outside and thought about what to do, I remembered a dream I had documented five days earlier. Here are quotes from the transcript:

"Some large plant, it's not quite a tree, but the stem is hard and woody . . ."

This is what a 9-foot limb *looks* like (even if, in literal terms, it's not a plant in itself).

"a significant portion of it has fallen down. "

This accurately reflects the waking event, since most of the limb had fallen, but a small part remained attached to the tree.

"As I'm looking at it I see someone . . . at the fence of Sam's yard that touches on the alley, right near their shed . . . and I think they're disposing of the same

plant somehow, or a similar one."

This pinpoints both the location and the type of tree involved. It's only from my tiny garden, where my Eugenia is, that I can see Sam's yard. And the fact that Sam's fence is bordered by Eugenia (in the form of a hedge), and "they're disposing of the same plant," provides further confirmation.

"I'm thinking—oh jeez, I'll have to cut it up into sections and put it at the curb, because it's big and needs to be disposed of. Do I want to hire someone or do it myself?"

As the event unfolded, this is exactly what went through my mind. I suspected that cutting up this six-inch diameter limb might best be accomplished with a chainsaw, which I don't own. It was a question that occupied me over the next few days as I made some exploratory cuts with a handsaw to see if I could handle the job myself.

Now back to an earlier point:

"As I'm looking at it I see someone at Sam's place . . . a person who's like a gardener . . . and I think they're disposing of the same plant somehow, or a similar one."

Though Sam's Eugenia is real, as I said, in the waking event no one was actually working on it, so this part is a miss.

However . . . as I stood over the chaotic mess the universe had just dropped in my lap, I scanned the surrounding area long and hard looking for help. So, while I'm not calling this a hit, my real-life *search*, if not its results, likely explains the worker in my dream. It expresses what I *wanted* to have happen. To see a chainsaw-wielding gardener would have been, at that particular moment, my ultimate fantasy.

Weighing the evidence.

With its five-day turnaround time, this dream is one of only six in my database that took longer than a day to come true. So if we judge it strictly from that standpoint, it's weaker than other cases.

But in one respect, a short delay actually *strengthens* the case. If the limb had fallen the same night as my dream, the skeptic could argue that I heard it snap while sleeping, and had the dream as a result. (From this standpoint, the ideal circumstance would have been a 36-hour interval, or thereabouts.)

As to the oddness factor, we've talked about how unusual the event was—a once-in-30-year happening. But what about the dream? It's important to keep in mind that the rarity of the dream itself also plays an important role in establishing the strength of a case.

Looking through my 241 recorded dreams, I see only two others that feature plants, so I can say with confidence that plants are not one of my recurring dream motifs. And those two dreams bear no resemblance whatsoever to this one.

So, as with the helicopter case (and others I'll be sharing), we have a once-in-a-lifetime dream matching up with a truly rare event. Once again we're looking at those two bullets shot from different guns. Though maybe this time, because of the five-day gap, we should say that they only grazed each other.

Could foreknowledge be a factor here?

My Eugenia was already mature when I moved to this house, and I suppose that as a tree ages, its limbs become heavier and more prone to breakage. So maybe the tree was ripe for such a mishap, and my awareness of the fact led to the dream.

But the idea that at some level I was concerned seems a bit far-fetched. After all, right up to the day in question, I had few worries about walking, sitting, lying, working, or exercising beneath that limb. Then, too, when I saw it lying there on the ground, I never experienced the slightest feeling of: well, it's finally happened as I always suspected it might.

And of course, such an explanation ignores the mystery of the near-perfect timing. Why did I have the dream just five days before the limb fell? Not even a tree specialist can predict such a mishap with any degree of accuracy.

Still, if I were to evaluate this case solely in terms of the likelihood of foreknowledge, it's not to the same standard of perfection as *Spinning Blades*. *Fallen Limb* is the only case in the book, really, for which even a *weak* argument can be made that I might have suspected (through conventional means) that the predicted event was about to happen. But such an argument would be just that, as I see it—weak.

Waiting for the other limb to drop.

Remember: it wasn't just the limb's falling that linked this dream to its matching event, but other specifics as well. This hand-in-glove fit was brought to mind recently when, four and a half years after the first limb came to a sad end, another met the same fate—the second in 35 years. But this time, the circumstances didn't match the dream nearly as well:

- The second limb was much smaller—not nearly big enough to make me wonder if I should pay someone to do the job, which, you'll remember, was my quandary in the dream and original event. This limb never even hit the ground (one end landed on a fence while the other remained attached) and thus wasn't creating a problem by blocking my path. And because my landlord has since hired a gardener, I could simply leave it for his next visit.

- In the dream, I described seeing someone at Sam's place while looking at the fallen limb. But this second limb was on the opposite side of the tree, and because of how and where it fell, there was no way I could see Sam's place while looking at it.

So it remains a fact that when the first limb snapped, it set in motion a fairly accurate, detailed re-enactment of my dream. And in the entire 35 years I've now been living in this house, nothing has happened to match the dream nearly as well as what took place five days after I woke up from it.

Still, is it possible that this juxtaposition of dream and waking event is just a coincidence?

Yes—when viewed as an isolated case.

But put yourself in my shoes. Suppose this sort of synchronicity follows in the wake of about a quarter of the dreams you keep track of. What then?

(More on this case in the Appendix.)

PART 3: HOW PRECOGNITION HIDES IN PLAIN SIGHT

8. The Barriers

If we all dream of the future night after night, why are so many of us unaware of the fact? It's an important question. Without a plausible explanation for it, you're likely to think one of two things: either psychic ability can't be real, or it's something *other* people have.

Let's begin with the most obvious of obstacles.

1. We forget nearly all our dreams instantly.

If you make the effort, you may be surprised at how many dreams you'll be able to recall. But you'll also begin to notice how, without that intention, even the most vivid dreams usually vanish without a trace almost as soon as you open your eyes.

This is the biggest factor, 25 years after my experiment began, that keeps me from observing precognition more often myself. It's a conclusion that's been forced on me by a simple fact—when I'm recording my dreams regularly, I may average a psychic dream per day; when I'm not, I can go months without noticing a single one.

I can't overstress the significance of that.

Still, we don't forget *all* our dreams—most of us remember the occasional one from time to time, even without trying. So why don't we see evidence for precognition more often in those instances?

For one thing:

2. Psychic dreams *feel* pretty much like ordinary ones.

I remember the first dream I had that struck me as though it might be precognitive.

Except for its astounding prescience, it seemed so very routine. In my innocence, I had assumed that psychic experiences, if real, would have a certain aura, some obvious quality that would make them stand out from others, but that hasn't proven to be true.

While it's a fact that some of my cases do involve dreams that were particularly intense or vivid, I've also had many *non*-psychic dreams that can be described that way.

3. A dream about the future with no verifiable specifics can easily be mistaken for a dream about the past.

Most of the actions and thoughts you'll experience today will be quite similar to those that occupied you yesterday. Getting up, washing, dressing, eating, working—if you had a legitimate precognitive dream last night about doing any of that, would you be able to distinguish it from a dream about the past?

Well, you might—but only if there were distinctive, out-of-the-ordinary specifics in the dream, details that characterize today, but not yesterday.

And that takes us back to the memory factor:

4. When we do remember a dream, we're likely to forget most of its details.

For a dream to seem psychic, it generally needs to mirror a real-life event in *multiple* ways. Just one or two correlations, unless they're truly striking, may not be enough to overcome our assumption that such things are impossible.

So the average person, whose only frame of reference may be poorly remembered dreams, is likely to say: "Sure, I dream a lot, and I've noticed some coincidences. But seeing the future? Give me a break!"

That's what I thought most of my life.

It wasn't until I started documenting my dreams in detail, and began to see the *full extent* of the parallels between them and waking events, that I realized I hadn't really been remembering my dreams—just bits and pieces of them.

But let's take this a step further. Suppose the memory of a dream does stay with you during the day, and with enough detail for you to notice more than one intriguing parallel with a real-life event. That will surely alert you to the fact that it might be precognitive, right?

Not necessarily. Remember:

5. Precognition seems impossible.

All our instincts tell us that precognition is just plain wrong. How can the future exist now? Being told that it does, is like hearing someone say that red is green, or *there* is *here*—it defies what we consider to be common sense.

Add to that intuition science's rejection of all psychic phenomena, and it's easy to see why we're likely to downplay any hint of precognition that might pop up. Why waste a moment speculating about something that's been officially declared bogus?

But let's say you're much less skeptical on the subject. For whatever reason, you're convinced that precognition is likely to be real. In that case, you'd be certain to grasp that this remembered dream with its interesting correlations is precognitive, right?

Once again—not necessarily. Because:

6. A dream may predict a future event but omit key aspects or change others, thus muddying the waters (until we take a closer look).

In presenting the Spinning Blades and Fallen Limb cases, I emphasized the similarities between dream and waking event.

But I've also been discussing differences (as you know if you've been reading the appendices). Besides trying to present the cases fairly, I've been doing so because those "misses" go to the heart of what we're talking about here.

Did you get that? I'm saying that mismatches, while seemingly weakening the case for precognition, are a key part of the story: they help to explain how we fail to see evidence for the phenomenon, even when it's staring us in the face.

A good example is *Fallen Limb*. While it provided some impressive details about what would happen five days later, I awoke from it unaware of a key point—I didn't understand that the event would involve a tree.

Similarly, in *Spinning Blades*, the dream didn't show me a bona fide helicopter (despite capturing its essence), and I was confused as to who was piloting the craft.

In both cases, if my attention had been focused on the differences rather than the whole picture, I might have seen only coincidence at work.

Considering all these factors, perhaps now you can understand why:

7. Often, it's only by assembling all the pieces of the puzzle that we can determine if precognition is involved.

If you try the experiment yourself, here's something to keep in mind. Most of the dreams I now consider to be precognitive seemed less than convincing at first. (J.W. Dunne makes the same point.) Typically, something will happen during the day and I'll think: "Hmmm . . . could this be a match for that dream I had last night? Naah—there aren't enough correlations."

But if I've documented the dream, I can go back to my recording, and maybe I'll see additional parallels. Or, in thinking about what just happened, I might gain further insights that answer other doubts I have about the strength of the evidence.

Eventually, I just might reach a point where I'll think: "You know what? This is one hell of a precognitive dream."

This sequence of events is common enough that it's probably accurate to describe it as the usual pattern these cases follow.

So am I massaging the evidence or getting to the truth?

Maybe you're thinking: "Bruce, doesn't what you just said tell you what's *really* happening? You want your dreams to be precognitive, and given enough time, you'll find ways to convince yourself that they are."

One counter-argument would be to point to the many instances in which dreamers report waking events that seem like literal or near-literal replays of their dreams. Because their visions are so true-to-life, these dreamers simply *know* they encountered the future as they slept, and no analysis is necessary. (I describe one such dream, the experience of someone I know well, in a later chapter. And before we're done, I'll provide a list of books brimming with such accounts.)

But while legitimate, that explanation won't do. I'm not suggesting my cases are meaningful because they confirm other people's experiences. I'm saying that despite being of the garden-variety, less dramatic sort, my dreams are persuasive in themselves—and particularly so in light of the one-in-four pattern we've discussed.

I'm suggesting that even though it may take some effort to get the full impact of dreams like mine, given the various camouflage factors (and there are others we've yet to discuss), that's understandable.

But you don't have to take my word for it. By presenting the facts of each case in detail, I've written and structured this book in such a way that you can decide for yourself if I'm making sense.

More to the point, I'm giving you the tools to explore your own dreams. Whether or not you resist the paranormal as much as I once did, that's where your real proof lies.

9. *The Round Object That Merged With a Flat Surface*: A Study in Similarities and Differences

I n this example, a bizarre vision predicted a single startling sentence I would later encounter in a blog. While several of the correlations are somewhat camouflaged, a thorough sniffing out of *all* the facts has convinced me that we're dealing here with a no-doubt-about-it glimpse of the future.

Note that this "dream" is actually a vision that came to me while meditating. I treat these as if they were dreams because they too involve images seen with eyes closed, which I then "wake up" from and immediately document.

Weirdness to the nth degree.

One morning just before 1 PM (morning for me, that is, since during this period of my life I was rarely going to bed before four), I visited Michael Prescott's blog, and saw a comment written by Jim E. Kennedy. Since it had been posted just hours earlier, there's no chance I had seen it before.

Included in his remarks was this:

> "In my first quantum mechanics class, the professor started by saying 'What we are going to study in this class is basically equivalent to **me throwing a tennis ball against this concrete wall and every now and then it goes through.'** " (Kennedy, 2014)

Well, that last part—the words I've bolded—caught my attention, and I stopped reading to try to imagine what it might look like. Putting myself in the professor's shoes, I pictured myself throwing the ball and visualized its flight in slow motion.

In particular, I dwelled on the moment the ball enters the wall silently without damaging it (as I presumed quantum physics would dictate), because that was the part I found irresistible. Here, in three stages, is what I saw in my mind's eye:

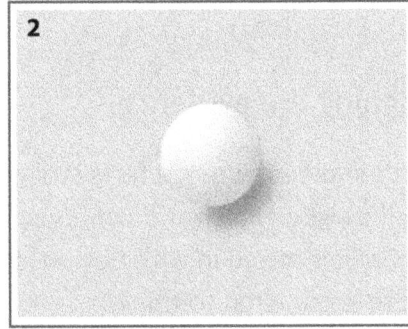

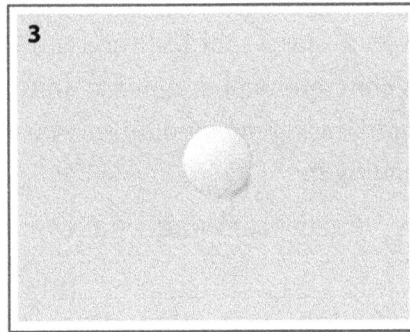

1. The ball makes contact and begins to enter the wall.

2. It looks smaller because its widest part is now inside the wall.

3. The ball has almost entirely disappeared.

As I was picturing this, I suddenly remembered a vision that had popped into my head while meditating about two and a half hours earlier. Here's part of my documentation for it.

> *"I was tossing disks, trying to get them to stick on the ceiling . . . more like circular pieces of paper or . . . thin material like that . . . maybe a couple of inches in diameter . . ."*

> *"I put that in the plural. It might have been just one I was trying to get up . . . certainly just one at a time."*

Weighing the evidence.

I don't know how these facts strike you, but I found the case underwhelming at first. It's a good illustration of how precognition manifests in my dreams—intriguing parallels mixed in with obvious differences, the net effect being that it's often hard to know what to think.

That is, until we take a closer look.

As you read on, keep in mind that the targeted event involves **"throwing a tennis ball against this concrete wall and every now and then it goes through,"** and that what I previewed during my meditation was not the sentence itself, but my *experience* while reading it.

In other words, my "dream" captured what I would later see as I visualized the ball's flight.

With that in mind, let's tally up the shared elements.

1. **I . . .** (Because I was picturing myself as the thrower, not the professor.)
2. **am throwing** . . .
3. **repeatedly** . . .
4. **a round object** . . . (My vision involves a disk or disks, but disks and balls are both round objects.)
5. **a couple of inches in diameter.** (A tennis ball is 2.7 inches.)
6. **I throw it at one of the large flat surfaces that enclose a room.** (Describes both ceilings and walls.)

7. **Sometimes, at least briefly, object and surface wed.** (As the ball contacts the wall in slow motion, it will seem at first to be *adhering* to it.)

OK. Note that as I've worded the correlations, each is literally true for both vision and waking event. A list of this sort is a great tool for ferreting out the common ground in these cases, without over- or underplaying it.

That last hit, in particular, is remarkable. And remember—rather than this being just one more detail, in both dream and event, it's the *central focus* of the exercise.

Now I ask you: how likely is it that within the space of two and a half hours, I would have a vision, and then encounter something in the real world, both of which include all those elements?

If precognition were not real, would you expect me to run into this sort of synchronicity one out of four times I document a dream?

But there's yet another parallel to discuss.

The hit that escaped me for over a year.

Here's the rest of the vision:

> *"The motion that I was using . . . it was like the disk was in the . . . like resting on my fingers, as my hand was hanging at my side. Resting on my fingers like on the inner surface of my hand, and it was kind of like an underhand heave up to the ceiling trying to get this disk or disks to, one at a time, stick flat on the ceiling."*

To grasp the significance of that, imagine that you're using the technique described above to toss a two-inch disk made of thin, paper-like material (as specified in the first paragraph).

Could you get it up to the ceiling? Not a chance. On leaving your hand, it would simply flutter down to the floor.

So what sort of object *might* you throw in that manner? It would have to be something firmer than paper. In point of fact, my careful description works perfectly as a guide to how to throw a ball.

(While other items would also fit the bill, remember: the object in my dream was round and roughly 2 inches across.)

Note, too, that the transcript details an underhand toss, which is surely how I would have thrown the ball in my visualization, owing to the short distance involved, and because that keeps the ball in my line of sight better than coming over the top with an overhand throw.

So we need to add another correlation:

- **The round object is thrown exactly as one would throw a ball underhand.**

Putting it all together.

Keep in mind that between documenting the vision and reading Jim's comment, just a little over two hours passed, and my notes tell me that it was one of the first things I read after meditating. The odds of seeing that vision, and then experiencing such a startlingly similar event so quickly, are slim indeed.

But I chose this example to illustrate the other side of the coin as well: how easily these dreams can slip by unnoticed. For perhaps you're beginning to understand how easy it would be to focus on relatively minor *differences* between dream and event (as I did here, at first), while downplaying correlations that beggar any attempt to use coincidence as an explanation.

All of which might lead one to ask: in weighing the evidence for psi, how do we, in fact, balance similarities against differences? Can one be said to be more important than the other?

Let's talk about that now.

(More on this case in the Appendix.)

10. The Lottery Number Concept

Some precognitive dreams are so true-to-life, it's almost as if the dreamer lives through an event once while sleeping, and then experiences it a second time while awake. I think of such cases as "classic," and a perfect example is Derek's dream in the chapter "How Fear Keeps Us In The Dark."

Garden variety precognitive dreams are different. As the waking event transpires, I don't usually feel as though I'm reliving something that's already happened.

Am I contradicting myself? If the difference between what I dream and what I later experience is that noticeable, why do I insist my dreams are psychic?

To help you understand my reasoning, here's a little thought experiment.

What really matters.

Imagine that we're sharing a meal, and I tell you I had an amazing precognitive dream the other day. I then proceed, for the next fifteen minutes, to describe in excruciating detail a dream in which a great many things happen, one of which is that I receive a letter.

I explain that I woke up from the dream, went out and bought a lottery ticket, and later that day learned that I won the jackpot.

And I say—how's *that* for seeing the future in my sleep!

Now, as it happens, you know me well, and because nothing about the dream sounds remotely like what's been going on in my life, you say: wow, winning the jackpot—that's fantastic, Bruce. But I don't get it. You dream about all that unrelated stuff, then you win the lottery—what's psychic about that?

And I say, "Whoops, I forgot to tell you—remember that letter I received in the dream? The winning lottery number was in it!"

Get it? Suddenly, all that matters is the number. If you compare that long dream to the entirety of my waking life afterwards, there may not be a single additional correlation. Every aspect of the dream other than the number may be pure fantasy.

But . . . against all the odds, there's that number to reckon with, that one verifiable, meaningful, sequence of digits from the future. And that changes everything.

The winning combinations in my dreams.

What I'm getting at is this: one out of four of the dreams I record contains a constellation of elements that is rare enough to be considered a lottery number of sorts, one that will match up perfectly with a "number" that is going to show up in my waking life—usually within hours or minutes. And in terms of proving precognition, *it matters little if everything else about the dream turns out to be fiction.*

For example, here again are the correlations in the *Round Object* case.

1. I . . .
2. am throwing . . .
3. repeatedly . . .
4. a round object . . .
5. about 2 inches in diameter.
6. I throw it as one would throw a ball underhand . . .
7. at one of the large flat surfaces that enclose a room.
8. The focus of the exercise is the fact that sometimes, at least briefly, object and surface wed.

This narrative neatly captures the essence of both vision and waking event, and despite the fact that I've slightly generalized items 4, 7, and 8, is unique and crisply defined—much like the number printed on a lottery ticket.

Now ask yourself: how likely is it that within the space of about two and a half hours, someone would have a vision, and afterwards find himself absorbed in a real-world narrative, both of which include all eight elements? (Don't forget to factor in the remarkable last item.)

Wouldn't such a feat be similar to dreaming a number containing many digits, and then shortly after awakening, stumbling on the identical number in some meaningful context?

And given the enormous odds against it, wouldn't the reality of such a synchronicity overshadow whatever "noise" or "garbage" might be present in the dream?

I think it would, and I believe that the same is true, for example, of the *Spinning Blades* case:

1. I see a man positioned below spinning helicopter blades.

2. He's seated out in the open, flying exposed to the elements.

3. He flies down a street-like corridor not far off the ground.

4. As he flies, the rotors nearly come into contact with power lines that surround him on both sides.

While #1 is common enough (seeing a pilot seated inside a helicopter would do the trick), #2 could easily add a few digits to our hypothetical lottery number. (Remember—in both dream and event he wasn't dangling from a rope like someone being rescued, but seated in a fixed position, behaving as a pilot or crew member would.)

If you then combine those with numbers 3 and 4 . . . well, have you ever seen that scenario in your entire life?

Neither have I—except for the day of the dream.

A sizable lottery number indeed, yet it was matched within hours.

To be clear . . .

So this is the sort of thinking I apply to all my dreams, though perhaps a qualification is in order. The analogy is far from perfect. For one thing, a real lottery ticket can't contain more than one jackpot-winning number, while a dream can conceivably match up with more than one event. (As unlikely as that seems, given the oddness of the dreams I document.)

On the other hand, the existence of an infinite variety of potential dream scenarios may well mean that likening a dream to a mere 7-or-so digit number *understates* its rarity.

In any event, I am by no means proposing a true mathematical framework for evaluating these cases. It's impossible to even begin to pin down numerically the odds of dreams coming true.

But since we're biased against seeing precognition, it's important to cut through the fog and come up with some guidelines, however imperfect, that can help us think logically about these things. And if what I've just described is not simple common sense, please drop me an email and tell me why.

When the dream itself *is* the lottery number.

Remember the hypothetical dream I concocted to help explain the lottery number concept? In one important way, the analogy is misleading. It doesn't do justice to my experiment because it presents an extreme scenario (for teaching purposes) that doesn't apply to my dreams.

The dream took fifteen minutes to narrate, and none of its elements, except for the lottery number, turned out to have any basis in reality.

But that's utterly different from my actual cases. I've included unedited transcripts in the appendices because I want you to see that for each dream, the correlations are central. The great bulk of those transcripts applies, in one way or another, to what actually happened soon afterward.

Bottom line: on the one hand I agree that there are obvious discrepancies in these cases. These variations are usually significant enough to keep me from experiencing a genuine sense of déjà vu. My precognitive dreams, like works of historical fiction, take real events (future ones, in this case) and *play* with them.

But the dreams nevertheless contain "lottery numbers," and they're not hidden in obscure corners. To a great extent, when you distill the dream scenarios down to their basic ingredients, the dreams *are* those lottery numbers.

And I win the jackpot one out of four times.

11. Metaphors: Revealers/ Concealers of The Paranormal

In comparing dreams to the events they predict, we've been talking about aspects or elements that match, and those that differ. And that brings us to the subject of metaphor, the meeting ground between the two.

A metaphor involves two things that are *similar*. In the meditation vision at the heart of the *Round Object* case, it's clear that the ceiling at which I was throwing a two-inch round thing represents, in the blog comment I was soon to read, the wall at which the tennis ball is thrown.

In that sense, "ceiling" is a metaphor for "wall."

Up to now, I've avoided words like metaphor and symbol for fear they might seem to introduce a note of vagueness to a subject (psi) that many feel is already fuzzy enough. But now I'll state the obvious: these cases often involve one thing standing in for another, and those surrogates are sometimes metaphors.

Now if metaphor seems to you a dubious form of evidence with which to prove something as controversial as precognition, then remember: I'm not talking about a figure of speech or poetic device. I use "metaphor" simply to describe something that my dreaming self has used to represent something else—something it resembles in ways that are impossible to deny.

For example (from the list of correlations for *Round Object*): **I throw it at one of the large flat surfaces that enclose a room.**

By simultaneously generalizing both "wall" and "ceiling" in this manner, I stripped away the metaphor and arrived at a *literal* correlation that is accurate for both dream and event. This gives us a better handle on the evidence and helps us to evaluate it fairly.

And with that understanding, we're ready to look at . . .

The two sides of metaphor.

1. Metaphors may provide clues to the presence of psi. In the *Fallen Limb* dream, I saw what I described as "some large plant, it's not quite a tree, but the stem is hard and woody." Since a limb is not actually a plant but *part* of a plant, you might say that my dream presented me with a metaphor.

And in *Spinning Blades*, the primitive "flying machine" in my dream serves a similar function. It stands in, as it turns out, for a real helicopter.

Since while experiencing the predicted events for those dreams I was alert to the potential for metaphor, I took seriously certain *approximate* correlations that came to mind in connection with the dreams. That, in turn, led to my uncovering other hits.

At that point, I suspected that precognition might be in play, and in each case, further study convinced me that it was.

2. Metaphor can *conceal* evidence for psi. The flip side of the above is equally important. On waking up from the *Fallen Limb* dream, I didn't grasp that what I had just seen was part of a tree. In that respect the dream fooled me, leaving the impression that the object in question was not a limb but an actual, independent, plant.

Which means that during all those years prior to grasping the reality of psi, it would have been easy for me to see the real-life fallen limb five days later, and even if it reminded me of the dream (which is unlikely, since I wouldn't have recorded it), to completely miss its significance.

Essentially the same is true with *Spinning Blades*.

So because metaphors have the potential to bring psi to our attention *or* hide it from us, we'll be referring to them often as we proceed.

Metaphor or misinterpretation?

There's a separate category of stand-in we need to discuss. The disk "a couple of inches in diameter" that appeared in my *Round Object* meditation obviously represents the tennis ball. But I don't think it's a metaphor. I think there's a better explanation. As I said in the Appendix to that chapter, I believe it was a result of my focusing on one isolated aspect of the scenario (the disk-like appearance of the nearly engulfed ball), while missing the larger context.

And here's another slant on misinterpretation. Sometimes I'll be reading an article, for example, and it will bring to mind a dream. I'll then quickly realize that I've misunderstood what I've been reading, and instead of picking up the author's true intentions, my dream captured my mistaken impression instead.

Dunne provides a perfect example of this sort of substitution. In 1902, he tells us in *An Experiment With Time*, he had a dream predicting the famous eruption of Mount Pelee, a volcano on Martinique, an island in the West Indies. He woke up believing that 4,000 people would die.

But as it turns out, that figure was based on a misreading:

"The number of people declared to be killed was not, as I had maintained throughout the dream, 4,000, but 40,000 . . . But, when I [originally] read the paper, I read, in my haste, that number as 4,000 . . . I did not know it was really 40,000 until I copied out the paragraph fifteen years later."

All of which confirms that rather than predicting objective facts per se, precognitive dreams often focus on the dreamer's inner life—his thoughts and feelings about what happens in the real world.

Taking seriously the meeting of psi and metaphor . . . while standing on solid ground.

So the deed is done—I've emerged from the closet and spoken the M word. And I've said that besides metaphors, there are other sorts of substitutions we also need to investigate.

In the meantime, if you happen to hear of some zealous skeptic who "reviews" my book without reading it, while perhaps making light of what he or she calls my attempt to prove the paranormal through metaphor—well, you can sit back and smile (even if I can't) because you know the truth: my evidence for psi consists exclusively of *literal* statements and facts.

That's important.

12. How Fear Keeps Us In The Dark

We've been talking about how it's possible to have verifiable dreams of the future yet be unaware of them. The explanations are many and varied.

But we've only scratched the surface. As we turn to the psychological factors, I'd like to kick off the discussion by getting personal. For about twenty years, the idea that psychic phenomena might be real posed a dilemma for me.

Not that I understood that. Back then, I would have laughed at the idea that the problem was mine. While it's true that the mere mention of the paranormal made me angry . . . well, isn't annoyance a reasonable response to claims so absurd they aren't even worth discussing?

And if you had pressed the matter further and suggested that perhaps my irritation revealed a touch of insecurity, I might have said: how can anyone be bothered by something that doesn't exist? (As in: "Angry!? I'm not angry!")

But psi *does* exist, and it's a hot button for many. Which brings us to the next item on our list of barriers to seeing precognition, a list we began several chapters ago.

This one is huge.

8. We may view the paranormal as a threat.

Few things are as sacred to us as our worldview—our personal understanding of who we are, where we're ultimately headed (if anywhere), and how to get there.

In particular, we each have our beliefs about where to turn in times of need. Some of us look to religion, others to therapy, science, philosophy, and so forth.

So it makes sense that if something comes along that's at odds with our beliefs, we might feel threatened. And for many, evidence for the paranormal can have precisely that effect.

It's not hard to see why. One of our key comforts is science, on whose accomplishments we are profoundly dependent. And science says flatly that psychic phenomena do not exist. So what happens if our experience tells us one thing, and our trusted experts another? Who or what are we to believe?

For many, to think that last night's dream might be precognitive opens the door to conflict and confusion. For if, in their ignorance, the brightest scientific minds are feeding us false information about the paranormal, how else might they be leading us astray? Can we trust science's pronouncements about our health care, medicines, and the safety of our foods? What about environmental concerns and possible dangers inherent in our new technologies?

In this respect, it's tempting to see a parallel between science and religion. In much the same way that, for centuries, most people saw the Church as their best hope for a better life, many today find it comforting to think of science as having the solutions to our most pressing concerns.

Or at least, they see science as having the best chance to *find* those answers.

So it makes sense that there are those who would prefer not to have heretics like me say that when it comes to fundamental aspects of reality such as precognition, mainstream science is wrong.

The inner turmoil that results when new information threatens our personal belief system is sometimes referred to as cognitive dissonance. To experience it feels uncomfortable, to say the least. And one way to steer clear of such unpleasantness is simply to refuse to look at any new, competing, data that comes along.

As I write this, recent headlines offer a dramatic example of this dynamic, an incident involving religion rather than science. When journalists are murdered for drawing cartoons that seem to make light of someone's faith, we see the extent to which some people will go to avoid contact with anything that conflicts with their way of looking at the world.

What's in *your* wallet?

Clearly, the specifics vary from person to person. We each have our own story, our own reasons for choosing to ignore or downplay certain inconvenient facts.

In contrast to the science-oriented, those who view the world through the lens of the Bible, Quran, or other text, may know that psychic abilities are real, but regard them as demonic, or at best, a distraction. (Maybe they feel that to grant a mere human such powers is to risk making him god-like or self-satisfied.)

In my case, the defining attachment was less towards science in general, than to a specific kind of psychotherapy that has been extremely helpful to me. My former therapist, a man who played a key role in my life for many years, is certain that psychic phenomena are an illusion, the product of neurotic thinking brought about by repressed emotional trauma.

And for almost two decades it never occurred to me that this bright light to whom I felt so grateful, might be wrong about *anything*. For him to be mistaken about psi would have meant he wasn't perfect. And where would that have left me? In my insecurity, I longed for an idealized mentor to hang onto, a heroic fig-ure free of the contradictions and ambiguities that plagued my own existence.

Might there be a similar dual-edged sword in your own life—a person, group, religion, or philosophy—that is in some ways your friend, and in others, an influ-ence that keeps you from seeing the larger picture?

All I can say is what's true for me—it took twenty years for me to gain what I needed from this therapist and through simply living my life, and to slowly put enough distance between us, so I could begin to see the world through my own eyes.

As it turns out, the discovery of my precognitive dreams was one of the factors that gave me the insight and motivation I needed to move on. Though for that to be possible—for psi to show up on my radar as even the faintest of blips—I first had to acknowledge the equally remote chance that my therapist was fallible.

And that's what happened. Because despite all my years of therapy, my life continued to be a struggle. As a result, after subscribing for two decades to some-one else's worldview in its entirety, I gradually began to understand that no one knows me better, or has greater insight into my needs and desires, than I do.

At that point, my need to inflate the importance of this man lessened, and I felt safe enough to begin the process of removing my blinders.

Eventually, psychic ability, together with the more spiritual outlook it implies, no longer posed a threat, and could thus been seen for what it was: a possibility worth considering—and a rather exciting one at that.

9. Experiencing the paranormal may trigger the fear that we're going insane.

Back in the early 1900's, when J.W. Dunne first became aware that some of his dreams were coming true, he worried that he might be losing his mind. It's understandable—little was known about precognition back then, so it must have been frightening to see the seemingly impossible invade his life.

In writing about Dunne recently, I pondered his dilemma and thought, "How interesting—but of course, it was different for me. In the 1990's, when I was opening up to my own psychic dreams, lots of New-Age enthusiasts were talking and writing about this stuff, so I hardly needed to fear for my sanity."

But then I remembered—just a few months before my startling discovery, I had been certain that all those people were nuts!

So you see, in the early days of my learning about precognition, a primary concern was indeed—am I losing it? For while I knew that others claimed to have such experiences, those were the very people to whom I had long felt superior— smarter, and less prone to comforting illusions.

We each have our own ideas about what it means to be sane. And as you now understand, for twenty years, the definition for me was simple—sanity is what my therapist says it is.

Clearly, by that measure, in 1992 I was headed the wrong way.

It took a long time for me to feel on solid ground. I'll have more to say about my process, and where I stand now, later in the book.

10. We may be frightened that our dreams—the terrifying ones— will come true.

While I myself am less worried, several friends tell me that the possibility of dreaming about a tragic event in advance frightens them. Some chronic precognitive dreamers, terrified of seeing yet one more sad prediction play out, have prayed for their dreams to cease, or even medicated themselves in the hope of preventing them.

Even those who merely *know* such dreamers can be affected. An example involves a ten-year-old boy, his amazing dream, and his father's response. (I'm disguising their identities for a reason I'll explain later.)

Without knowing about my interest in the subject, the boy, whom I know extremely well and have every reason to trust—let's call him Derek—once told me that he often found himself reliving his dreams. He then illustrated the point with something that had happened earlier that day.

When I told him I found such experiences fascinating, he said, "How about bad dreams? Can they come true, too?"

I didn't want to scare him, but I didn't want to lie. So I said sometimes they can. But I then explained that there was a silver lining: a person may dream of an unfortunate event, and thanks to the dream, be able to alter the experience when it actually comes to pass, thus preventing the worst.

Instantly, he perked up and said: yes, that happened to me. He said he dreamt he was playing tetherball at school. In the dream, the chain attached to the ball snapped and the ball hit him in the head, causing him to trip and fall.

As he lay on the ground, a playmate accidentally pushed another kid towards Derek's right side. This child had blonde hair and wore a green shirt, and landed on Derek's arm, breaking it.

Well, the dream came true the next day, *including all those details*—but with a difference. Remembering the dream, he rolled to the side and avoided the child to his right, who landed where Derek's arm had been the moment before.

The blonde kid turned out to be Derek's friend Robert, and Derek's father told me that fair-haired kids were few and far between in Derek's class.

When I asked Derek if he remembered any other details that might make the case even more convincing, Derek said that in the dream, it was windier and the green shirt was fuzzier.

That last part tells me a lot—his memory of both dream and event was sharp. Equally important, he wasn't about to exaggerate the similarities just to please me.

A parent's skepticism.

Even if the breaking of the tetherball chain were the only correlation, the dream would be an intriguing one. But all those other specifics—not to mention the spectacular, apparently injury-preventing aspect—make this a powerful account indeed.

As I've said, I consider my own precognitive dreams garden-variety—the evidence is sufficiently camouflaged that a closer look is often required to be certain that psi is genuinely at work.

This case is different, though—no metaphors, and only minor variations. Up until the stunningly different ending, it's as though Derek had already experienced the event beforehand.

But here's the thing. Derek's father (I'll call him Steven), was not in the least impressed, a reaction I found startling. Steven doesn't believe in precognition, and sees nothing remarkable or meaningful in his son's experience.

So what's happening here? How can anyone hear such a story from someone with no apparent motivation to lie—hear it from one's own child, no less—and fail to be interested? Is Steven dense? Is he a remote and uncaring father?

Hardly, on either account. He and I have talked on a wide range of subjects and I know him to be quick and knowledgeable. His rapport with his kids is a delight to see.

I *like* Steven.

But as I see it, in this one respect, he behaves and thinks irrationally. And when I pressed him to explain why he dismisses Derek's experience, he had little to say.

Except, that is, for one thing. He confided that he finds precognition "creepy" because, like others I've mentioned, he's terrified about the possibility of dreaming something horrific that might later come true.

Now I'm not saying that this fear by itself fully explains Steven's reaction. But fear is a powerful motivator. And if you prefer not to believe in something as controversial as psi, it's easy to latch on to countless excuses not to, many of which can seem quite rational.

In any case, feelings need to be respected, which is why I've camouflaged identities here. After my initial prodding, I'm no longer interested in shoving this evidence in Steven's face.

The irony is that if Derek had himself been predisposed to dismiss such dreams, he may well have ended up with a broken arm.

11. To take our precognitive dreams seriously is to risk being judged by others.

The following post from a 12-year-old girl appeared on a question-and-answer forum, under the heading "I see the future in my dreams. How do I tell my family, and will they think I'm a freak?"

> "I see about a 4-5 second vision while I'm dreaming. But when I wake up, I forget it. Once the event comes, (it could be a day later, or a week, or even a month or a year later) I suddenly remember everything, and no matter what I do to stop it from happening, everything still happens like I dreamed it would. This happens frequently, and it started around five years ago when I was seven. I think I want to tell my family but [I'm] scared they might think I'm delusional or a freak, or that they won't believe me . . . Any advice??" (Anonymous, 2015)

I feel for this girl—her fear is not that she'll be looked at askance by some unknown "others," but by her own family. (Her story also shows how the phenomenon varies from person to person. I, for one, have never forgotten a dream for months and then recalled it.)

Given the power of her experiences, it's not surprising she needs help. At least we garden-variety psychics have the luxury of being able to ignore the less dramatic evidence in our own dreams, something we do largely subconsciously. We thus avoid being judged, while simultaneously escaping the painful cognitive dissonance that cries out from that letter.

To give another example, it's common knowledge that revealing an interest in psi can be professional suicide. If you're a doctor, for example, or an attorney, scientist, or other professional looking to further your career, hosting a blog on the paranormal might not be the smartest of moves.

And in this presidential election year here in the U.S., this comes to mind:

imagine what would happen if a reporter dug up an essay written by one of the candidates entitled "Psychic Dreams—Their Role in My Life." Can you picture the headlines?

In a nutshell

Considering the enormous fear our paranormal abilities can trigger, it's no surprise that many of us find it easier to remain blissfully unaware of them. And with mainstream science leading the way, denial can seem downright logical.

The point being: while fear may not be able to stop us from having a psychic dream, it can certainly keep us from recognizing it for what it is.

13. The Ocean in Which We Swim

The student fish says to the philosopher fish, "What's this ocean you keep talking about?"

Since we're immersed in our culture's biases from the moment we're born, its assumptions are largely invisible to us, yet they profoundly influence all our thoughts and actions. Here are yet two more reasons we're blind to precognition, beliefs or attitudes that are so prevalent, we rarely stop to question them.

12. We assume that dreams have little meaning.

Dreams are often explained as random firings of brain cells for the purpose of releasing tension accumulated during the day—hardly an inspiring perspective on an activity to which we devote so much time and energy.

But it's not just science that's dismissive. This belittling of our nighttime visions permeates our entire culture. Whether we're talking to our children or comforting ourselves, the catch-phrase is "it's only a dream," as if nothing of importance happens after our head hits the pillow.

We regard even sleep with disdain, and admonish each other, in one context or another, to "wake up!" After all, everyone knows that it's only when we open our eyes and begin to use our powers of reason that we can do worthwhile things like conduct business and carry out science-as-usual.

So it's through the lens of this bias that we view our dreams, and we're quick to reject the possibility that they have much to teach us.

Case in point. I recently needed to view an old Phil Donahue show to refresh my memory about the televised waking event at the heart of an older case. So I called the clip licensing department at a major studio. The woman in charge was extremely helpful given how little profit this transaction was likely to generate.

Then she asked the reason for my research. When I told her I was writing a book on dreams (not even mentioning the psychic part), she said simply: that won't do.

When I asked why, she said she needed to write the request in such a way as to motivate others in her department to not only track down this obscure video, but also to clear any legal hurdles that might keep it from the public. A book about dreams, she said, wouldn't seem important enough.

Ouch.

(I ended up getting the video—maybe she was influenced by the article I later sent her that included an impressive list of scientific discoveries made with the help of dreams.)

A culture with one eye closed.

Think of it this way: to say that precognition is real but best observed in the dream state would be to give considerable importance to our nocturnal visions. It would be to grant, even if only in this respect, more authority to dreams than ordinary consciousness. And in our culture, that's taboo.

Imagine, for example, a candidate for president of the United States discussing political insights gained through his or her dreams. How would that go over in the press? (I've used the presidential example twice now. What we demand to hear or not hear from our leaders speaks volumes.)

Now compare that to a situation which has existed in many, or even most, societies throughout history. Pharaohs, emperors, Native American chiefs, and so forth, were often *expected* to make decisions based, in part, on their visions and dreams. Not to mention shamans, those masters of non-ordinary consciousness who figure so prominently in indigenous cultures throughout the ages.

So it's clear that we've been talking about the ocean in which *we* swim, here in the 21st century, rather than the only frame of reference, or even, over the millennia, the most popular.

Michael Harner points out that science is *cognicentric*. In seeking the truth, he says, mainstream science uses but a single mode of consciousness—rational, intellectual, thought.

I ask you then: as you and I wake up from a dream that has somehow shaken us, and wonder if it might truly be worth taking note of, how can we not be influenced, even if subconsciously, by science's dismissal of the entire subject?

13. Randomania

As you've noticed, I'm constantly reminding you that one in four of my recorded dreams comes true. It's not that I'm forgetful or think you're not paying attention. I do it to counter what parapsychologist David Luke calls randomania—our habit of attributing unexplainable events to the workings of chance.

Here's an example. In the early stages of writing this book, I shared my experiment with my neighbor Arthur, a psi skeptic. Only after discussing in depth with him the one-in-four result and how I arrived at it, did I present to him one of my cases.

When I finished he immediately replied, "Interesting. But you know, out of a million dreams one is bound to come true."

Get it? Just moments earlier Arthur and I were talking about how my experiment is designed to counter such objections, and at that time he agreed, at least in principle, that a one-in-four result seemed meaningful.

So if he had now said, "You know, Bruce, despite that pattern you're claiming to see . . . " and then offered a counter-argument, his reaction would have made sense. But he didn't. He simply repeated the standard skeptical response, as if our earlier talk had never happened. His remark was canned and automatic rather than relevant.

So was Arthur just being forgetful? I don't think so. What he was vulnerable to, in that moment, was randomania: the subject of psi comes up, curiosity and reason fly out the window, and bulldozing over all other considerations is the urge to quash the discussion by any means possible.

I like this description by Michael Prescott. Following Roger Knights' practice, he's using a capital S to indicate an especially committed skeptic:

A Skeptic encountering evidence of the paranormal is like the stereo-typical woman in a movie farce who discovers a spider in her hair. Does she pause to calmly assess the situation? No, she starts batting wildly at her head, screaming, "Get it off me!" In this state of mind, even the most intelligent and knowledgeable person will be hard pressed to think logically. Panic makes anyone stupid. (Prescott, 2015)

Maybe "panic" seems like too a strong a word to you. After all, my conversation with Arthur was low-key and he didn't seem frightened. But my guess is that his "forgetting" my statistic is just the sort of small, unconscious, decision we make countless times a day, a tactic that keeps our anxiety—our level of cognitive dissonance—in check.

(To be clear, I wouldn't call Arthur a skeptic with a capital S. In fact, he told me about an extraordinary dream of his own, one he seems to feel certain was genuinely precognitive. I say "seems," because despite describing his experience with conviction and wonder, he evidently remains agnostic on the subject.)

Randomania and this experiment.

At this point some readers may be thinking—randomania? Give me a break! How about the opposite? What about our tendency to see patterns where none exist? Our urge to find meaning in every coincidence? (Apophenia, as it's called.)

Well, I'm aware of that too. In talking about my dreams, I often run into people who seem eager to embrace every psychic, supernatural, or spiritual claim that comes down the pike. Because our attitudes are so at odds, I'm frankly uncomfortable discussing psi with them.

Those who are (in my opinion) credulous see no need for an experiment like mine. I'd rather talk to the deeply skeptical. I've been in their shoes, and there's at least the possibility he or she might come to appreciate why I feel so passionately about this project—in part, because dreams lend themselves to countering randomania better than other types of psychic experiences.

Here's what I mean. Let's say you observe an apparent anomaly of some sort. Maybe you have an especially vivid thought about someone, and seconds later, they call you for the first time in thirty years. You say to your friend the skeptic, isn't this interesting? And he replies, do you know about the law of large numbers?

And what can you say other than "it seems to happen pretty often!"

"Confirmation bias," says your friend. "You're remembering all the times it happens, and forgetting all the times it doesn't."

Well, for me it's different. I can say: no, I know exactly what percentage of my dreams come true. Large numbers have nothing to do with this. And by the way, I know how *long* they take, too.

Since dreams can be conveniently documented and tallied on awakening, they lend themselves to mathematical reckoning, and I've taken advantage of that.

So is this experiment a cure for randomania? You'll have to decide that for yourself. But for me personally, there's no doubt it continues to play a key role in how I see myself and my world.

PART 4: SEALING THE DEAL WITH DREAMS THAT COME TRUE IN MINUTES

14. Two Vast Pools? Answering the Skeptic's Main Objection *(The Student Loan)*

ince I've titled Part Four "Sealing the Deal," I want to stress once again that I'm aware of the limitations of a mere book. And I understand them, in particular, with regard to proving the statistic to which I so often refer: my one-in-four success rate. So my goal is simply to show how I proved precognition to myself, and encourage you to explore your own dreams.

OK—back to our story.

The skeptic's refrain.

"Bruce, you're seeing the law of large numbers at work. That's all."

This is shorthand for what I call the *two vast pools theory*. It says that given (a) countless dreams, and (b) a virtually infinite supply of waking events, striking correlations are bound to pop up from time to time.

But the thing is, in my experiment, "countless dreams" has been reduced to four, since that's all it takes, on average, for evidence of precognition to turn up.

And as to the supposedly enormous pool of real-world experiences, consider this: 39% of my precognitive dreams came true within an hour.

Six took less than five *minutes*.

Do you see the further damage these small-interval cases do to the two vast pools theory?

Here's another example from my archives. While the actual time involved was twelve minutes, in practical terms it was considerably less.

Teacher's setting me straight about a student loan? You gotta be kidding.

This case was set in motion by an obvious similarity that brought the dream to mind while reading an online news story. Since other correlations were better hidden, though, if the dream had taken a while to come true, I probably wouldn't even have bothered to follow up on that first clue.

But . . . it took almost no time at all. This is nearly an instant match. Since reading the article was virtually the first thing I did after making my recording, the supposedly vast pool of potential matching events was almost empty, and that changes everything.

Here are some quotes from the dream:

> *"I'm talking with . . . it's either Mr. Plumley [my piano professor from my college years] or some similar figure. I have a copy of a score, some piano music, and I've evidently just finished working on a piece in the book . . . he's claiming that I borrowed it from him, and I'm thinking that it's mine.*
>
> *Now I'm just a bit peeved that he's making a big issue of this because I've obviously had the book . . . for so long that it has all my fingering in it . . ."*

(Fingering refers to numbers penciled in by a pianist as an aid to playing.)

After documenting the dream, I went to the bathroom, checked my email (there was only one, from PBS), went to CNN.com, and immediately began reading an article entitled "Who Won the Republican Debate?" I hadn't seen the debate nor did I know anything about what was said.

About three minutes into reading the article, I see: "In one of Rubio's strongest and most memorable lines of the night, **he said: '. . . Who is Hillary Clinton to lecture me about repaying students** [sic] **loans?'** " (Setmayer, 2015)

Understandably, the words I've bolded reminded me of the dream I had just finished recording. And though I wasn't all that impressed at first (have you heard this before?) I started tallying up the correlations, and by now, I've uncovered about a dozen.

If you're wondering how so many parallels can be drawn from just one sentence, it's because the waking event consists of more than just Rubio's remark—

we have to factor in the common knowledge I *brought* to it: Clinton and Rubio are in the same field; she's older and more experienced; a student loan is a long-term transaction; Rubio had to pay off such a loan himself—all these well-publicized facts shaped my reaction, and are just as much a part of the event as the article itself.

(Note to ebook readers in particular: The *Evidence-at-a-Glance* supplement will be particularly useful as you read the following commentary, since you'll need to keep referring to both dream and event in detail.)

1. **A long-term loan to a student,** (By the end of the transcript, it's clear that I did actually borrow the book from my teacher.)

2. **the need for which has essentially ended,**

3. **is the cause of a conflict between two people in the same field.** (Like Mr. Plumley, teaching piano has been my primary occupation.)

4. **One is older, more experienced, and acts as teacher.**

5. **The younger is the student and borrower.** (Student seems appropriate for Rubio since he's being lectured to, and borrower also fits because he implies—and it's well-known—that he's had the experience of paying back his own student loan.)

6. **The disagreement has been triggered by the older person's stance on the return of the borrowed item.**

7. **The situation is reported to us directly by the younger person,** (This is but one of many possibilities—the message could have been delivered by the older person, a neutral observer, an acquaintance of either one, through a scene in a movie or novel, expressed as common knowledge, etc.)

8. **who expresses his annoyance.**

I list several additional hits in the Appendix.

Wordplay.

Now maybe you're puzzled by this one. After all, in comparing dream to event, there are countless differences between the two scenarios—quite possibly they outnumber the similarities.

And yet . . . there *are* those correlations: loan, student, teacher, mutual profession, disagreement—all these concepts and more are unquestionably shared elements. It's as if my dreaming self thought: "Won't this be cool—I'm going to take the words from Rubio's sentence and use them in an entirely different context. I'm going to create a completely new story out of them."

Because clearly, that's what happened. From this perspective, "Who is Hillary Clinton to lecture me about repaying students loans?" makes perfect sense as the dream's inspiration. Everything about it, including aspects of the relationship between the two people, and the speaker's exasperation, has been touched on, albeit treated in entirely new ways, within the dream.

Here's another way to put it: while I wouldn't say the case involves puns in the conventional sense, it does resemble that sort of wordplay by assigning contrasting meanings to the same words. The "pun" here, as suggested by my earlier subheading, is on the entire thought: "Teacher's setting me straight about a student loan? You gotta be kidding." Take another look at both dream and event and you'll see how nicely that captures the essence of each.

I see the same dynamic at work in many of my dreams—often in the form of puns that are both clear and ingenious.

Does this surprise you? If so, I can relate. Back when I was first beginning to explore the psychic side of my dreams and stumbled on what seemed to be witticisms linked to future events, I thought I must be mistaken. But by now, I'm confident the puns are real. Sometimes they're verbal, and sometimes, visual, or even tactile. But they're always unmistakable, and in later chapters, I'll share some examples.

I'll also show how a certain category of dream with which most readers will be familiar—I call them lead-up dreams—leave no doubt whatever that the linking of dreams to waking events through double entendres is common.

Now if you think the whole idea of proving psi while pointing to metaphors and puns is questionable, or if you fail to see the strength of this specific case, I have a challenge for you. Don't even think about wordplay. Just go over that list of correlations again. Isn't each and every one *literally* true for both dream and waking event? (And there are other hits in the appendix.)

The answer, of course, is yes. So I ask you: how does such a complex synchronicity turn up just moments after recording that dream? How did that "lottery number" get matched so quickly?

Staying clear about what matters.

Though this case is missing the spectacularly odd content we saw earlier—there's no flying machine with outdoor passenger, once-in-30-year tree mishap, or merging of objects—the sheer number of hits, and above all, the timing, make up for its relative ordinariness.

I can't stress this strongly enough: other than getting out of bed, setting up my laptop in another room, and glancing quickly at a few emails, reading that article was the *first thing I did* after having the dream and recording it.

Do you see how that multiplies the strength of the evidence exponentially? Like the one-in-four statistic, it's the sort of fact that proves psi, but that randomania will do its best to keep us from seeing, fully absorbing, and pondering.

I hope you'll do all three.

Do I manipulate events to get the results I want?

This seems a good opportunity to address another reservation some readers may have.

Imagine, if you will, that you're conducting an experiment. You just had a dream about the loan of some music and a disagreement related to it, and you'd love it to come true, preferably within minutes. (May as well state the obvious here.)

And here's my point. If you were trying to nudge the process along, would you then head straight for an article entitled "Who Won the Republican Debate"? I mean, who would expect to find a match there, for a dream like this?

No one, obviously. I clicked on it for one reason only—I was eager to find out what those silly conservatives were up to.

I trust that you see how important this is. Because what I just described is true for all my cases. I wake up from a dream, narrate it onto my iPod, and while waiting to see if anything turns up, I simply live my life.

And that's been my approach from the start, because preference or no, my primary motivation has always been to get at the truth. If I modify my behavior in the slightest in the hope of moving events in the desired direction, how can I trust my findings?

Of course, if I had seen a story titled "Teacher sues student in dispute over music score," I would have clicked on that first. But that wouldn't be manipulation—just following up on an already striking correlation (and irresistible headline).

In a nutshell.

We began the chapter by talking about two allegedly enormous pools that skeptics rely on to dismiss precognition. But as you know, in terms of my experiment, the one containing dreams has been narrowed down to just four.

And now, thanks to the 39% of my precognitive dreams that came true within an hour, we see that the supposed abundance of potential matching events may also be a red herring.

The dream we've just been exploring is a prime example. Because after recording it, reading the CNN article was virtually the first thing I did. So what does that say about the "ocean" of possibilities that might make coincidence a reasonable explanation?

(More on this case in the Appendix.)

15. More on That Shrinking Events Pool

Dreams that come true in minutes aren't the only problem for the it's-just-coincidence approach to debunking psi. As we take a closer look at how this argument fares when applied to other cases, you'll see what I mean.

When more than minutes are involved . . .

The skeptic says, "Bruce, let's talk about a dream that takes several hours to come true. From the instant you wake up, you have the opportunity to latch onto *any of the countless things you see or experience,* and convince yourself that the dream has predicted it. That's a lot of fruit for the picking."

Not necessarily. Remember when I said that I weed out dreams that focus on the sorts of things that happen all the time? Since such dreams have no value in proving or disproving precognition, in terms of the experiment, they're irrelevant.

Well, the same is true for routine *events.* As it turns out, to truly understand these cases, it's essential that we remove generic experiences from the equation entirely.

Think of it this way: on a typical day I get out of bed, fold up my futon, put away my blanket and pillow, take a shower, brush my teeth, dress, and do my yoga routine.

Now unless something unusual happens while I'm engaged in one of those acts, wouldn't you agree that none of them is potentially the target of a provable precognitive dream? And that none is therefore available for me to "latch onto"?

Which means that during that time—45 minutes, perhaps—I would have had no opportunity whatsoever to try to match my hypothetical dream.

(Note that I live alone, which eliminates the sorts of surprises a spouse or child might introduce into otherwise routine events. Also, I don't include eating breakfast in that list, because I'm online then.)

All that time passed, and the skeptic's argument about "every single thing you see or experience" carries no weight.

The same applies to time I spend preparing meals, washing dishes, doing the laundry, paying bills, cleaning my apartment, and watering and fertilizing my garden. (Sorry about these lists—I can't think of any other way to drive this easy-to-overlook point home.)

This is why, in determining the interval between dream and event, I don't include the time I spent making the recording. Only once has a dream predicted something that took place as I was documenting it.

Back to those pools . . .

What we're talking about in this chapter is what I call the *pool of potential matching events.* Like the dreams pool, it provides, supposedly, a wealth of possibilities to which randomaniacs like to draw our attention.

But we need to be wary of being taken in by mirages. As I trust you're beginning to understand, we need to get clear about what belongs in this pool and what doesn't. Otherwise it will seem bigger than it is, and we'll be biased towards seeing coincidence at work.

That's why we need to think in terms of events that are truly relevant because they're provable.

And here's something else to consider—it's not just the commonplace we need to eliminate:

Inner-oriented activities like thinking and writing also have to be tossed out.

More and more, I've become a full-time author. Yet none of my precognitive dreams has ever targeted the countless hours I spend writing. Nor is that likely to change.

Why? Because writing is an *interior* act. To prove that an experience was predicted by a dream, it has to have been triggered externally by someone or something that provides information to which I had no prior access.

If I dream of writing about a polka-dotted penguin, and months later I actually do, it can always be argued that the seed for that breathtaking inspiration was in my mind all along. Or that the motivation came from the dream itself.

To slightly broaden the point, how much of your day is devoted to simply *thinking*? How often might you be described as largely oblivious to your surroundings, dwelling instead on feelings or ideas that are purely internal?

Introvert that I am, such moments account for a sizeable chunk of my life. And for the reasons I've given, none of that time—whether I'm philosophizing, reminiscing, anticipating, or planning—figures into my provable events pool.

Don't get me wrong: thoughts and feelings are central to these cases. But only when they're directed towards fresh, unexpected, external stimuli.

The shrinking events pool and its effect on the experiment.

So what does all this mean in terms of evaluating the evidence in our dreams? Here's a good example.

One day I took a nap in the evening and woke up at 8:30 PM, right in the middle of an interesting dream. I recorded it, and immediately got back to the writing I had been doing earlier.

After several hours of focused work, I cooked a meal. I then turned on the TV, sat down to eat, and within fifteen minutes, at 1:10 AM, I was watching a scene from a movie that, to my delight, matched the dream beautifully.

Now it might seem that the *interim* (the interval between recording the dream, and the moment it came true) was about four and a half hours.

But to leave it at that would be misleading. Because other than the 15 minutes I spent watching the movie before that scene came on, nothing I did during those several hours was likely to lead to a provable precognitive dream.

For our purposes, you could almost say that the long hours I spent writing never happened. So while the dream in question isn't literally one that came true in minutes, do you see that, in terms of the experiment, it comes very close to belonging to that category?

To each his own.

To be clear: what I'm presenting in this chapter are general principles that apply to anyone who tries an experiment like mine. But we each need to view these facts in the light of the specifics of how we live, and with respect to each individual dream.

For many of us, the sort of work we do will be a deciding factor. That's certainly true for me.

Specifically, only one of the cases in my database stems from the countless hours I've spent giving piano lessons, although that was my main profession for many years. In general, the work is too repetitive to provide fodder for my experiment.

Don't misunderstand—it's likely that I frequently *do* dream in advance about teaching. Because often, while with a student, I'll suddenly notice that some part of me has drifted back to a dream I had the previous night. Its content will usually be too vague or generic, though, to know for sure if precognition is involved.

Similarly, I've spent hundreds of hours producing piano tutorial videos. None has ever led to a documented psychic dream. Combine all this with what I've said about writing, and we've just accounted for virtually all the hours I spend making a living.

My provable events pool is disappearing fast.

So what's left?

Perhaps you're beginning to see why my precognitive dreams so often involve media-related experiences. My sleeping self seems most interested in picking up moments from the future when I'm relaxed and engaged in activities involving unexpected, engaging, and often highly unusual, scenarios.

And what fits the bill better than time spent reading or watching the tube?

Caveat emptor.

The argument I'm making in this chapter is, at times, a subtle one. I look forward to feedback from you, my readers, as to how it jibes with your own experience.

And as I've said, my understanding of what I'm calling the events pool is based on *my* life. Living alone, as I do, eliminates the sorts of surprises a spouse or child might introduce into otherwise routine events.

(A related fact: nothing pleases me more than silence, so I rarely have TV, radio, or music on in the background, further reducing opportunities for the unexpected to intrude.)

What I know for sure.

I recently saw the following response, in Scientific American, to an article on psi:

> "Given the mind bogglingly large number of possible human perceptions and experiences and that the nature of the mind is to perceive correlations whether causal or not, it is not surprising that there are [a] fair number of quite surprising coincidences." (Commenter and date not known.)

While the writer wasn't talking about precognition specifically, his argument is precisely the one skeptics use to refute it.

But here's the thing. If I have a dream, then spend four hours deeply immersed in writing, and then, within minutes of turning on my TV, see a scene that mirrors the dream, does it make sense to talk about a "mind-bogglingly large number of possible human perceptions and experiences"?

Obviously not. And given my lifestyle, what I just described is typical, to varying degrees, of virtually all my cases.

As I've said, you'll have to see how these principles apply in practice to you and your dreams. But speaking for myself, I'll say this: while at least 39% of my cases are hard to dismiss because of how quickly the dream comes true (within an hour), even ones that take longer aren't nearly as amenable to the law of large numbers as skeptics think.

16. Lead-Up Dreams: A Punny Thing Happened This Morning As I Was Waking Up

We've been talking about cases in which the predicted event arrives in just minutes. But to leave the matter there would be misleading, because many dreams seem to come true *instantly*. I call these cases lead-up dreams (LUD's) for a reason that will soon be obvious.

Whether they're precognitive is hard to prove. However, by knowing what to look for, I think we can arrive at a fair degree of certainty—and maybe even close the deal entirely. (Especially given the nearly identical examples I'll be presenting in the *next* chapter.)

But psychic or not, the category of experience we're about to explore strongly supports the argument I've been making, and in more ways than one.

Perhaps the most famous lead-up dream was recorded by the 19th-century French scholar Louis Ferdinand Alfred Maury. Maury dreamt himself a victim of the Reign of Terror, the period in Revolutionary France during which citizens deemed enemies of the state were routinely guillotined.

> *"I was slightly indisposed and was lying in my room; my mother was near my bed . . . [in the dream] I am present at scenes of massacre; I appear before the Revolutionary Tribunal; I see Robespierre, Marat, Forquier-Tinville, all the most villainous figures of this terrible epoch; I argue with them; at last, after many events which I remember only vaguely, I am judged, condemned to death, taken in a cart, amidst an enormous crowd, to the Square Of Revolution; I ascend the scaffold; the executioner binds me to the fatal board, he pushes it, the knife falls . . ."* (Maury, 1865)

At that precise moment, Maury awakens, and . . .

"I feel on my neck the rod of my bed which had become detached and had fallen on my neck as would the knife of the guillotine. This happened in one instant, as my mother confirmed to me." (Ibid.)

The "rod" was presumably part of a canopy, a common feature of beds of that era. Maury's last sentence shows that there was no warning—nothing that might have alerted him, while sleeping, to what was about to happen.

Lead-up dreams are fairly common; I had one myself back in the days when I was certain precognition was pure nonsense. Though I've forgotten its precise content, as with Maury's dream, mine led up to, and "explained," a sensation I would feel on awakening—in this case, the touch of an insect landing on my skin.

I remember thinking, what in the world just happened? How could I dream about something that would occur *later,* even if only by a fraction of a second? I ended up assuming that I must have been mistaken as to the sequence of events.

Psychic or not?

Originally, I planned to say that lead-up dreams are precognitive and leave it at that. But my friend Cal Harris said something to me recently that has somewhat softened my stance.

We were talking about the usual non-psychic explanation for these experiences, namely, that the dream only *seems* to precede the event. According to this theory, Maury felt the canopy strike his neck, and then instantly dreamed a scenario incorporating that sensation.

I said such a hypothesis seems flawed because lead-up dreams are often so elaborate. Take Maury's, for example—how can such a detailed, lengthy narrative be squeezed into a fraction of a second?

Then he reminded me of something I already knew, but perhaps wasn't taking seriously enough. It sometimes happens that in car crashes, falls from great heights, and similar situations, time can seem to slow down to a startling degree, and we can have a remarkably full experience within a very brief span.

So maybe the same can happen in a dream. If so, that would muddy the waters and leave the psychic status of lead-up dreams up in the air.

But then I discovered a fascinating account on Anthony Peake's online forum.

If there are enough cases like the following, as shared by Jason Taverner, perhaps we can clear up the matter once and for all. Jason says:

> "I dreamed of a portable projector screen (the type that folds up and sits on a tripod . . .)
>
> The closed projector screen, along with tripod, was toppling over, falling in slow motion, in blackness. It seemed to take an age to hit the ground, when it finally did I heard an almighty crash and was awoken, startled and frozen in pitch black darkness, wondering what had happened. The next thing I knew my mother had switched on the light and it turned out my reasonably large, wooden framed mirror had fallen off my bedroom wall." (Taverner, 2008)

The similarities between this case and Maury's (and mine) are obvious. But there's a difference—James was roused from sleep not by a sensation, but a noise. And since he woke up in "pitch black darkness," he had no way of immediately knowing what created that ruckus, a fact he stresses:

> "I just remember hearing the loud noise and, regardless of the dream, being totally clueless as to what was going on. It was only after the light was turned on (and therefore presumably AFTER the dream had been imposed) that [I] knew what had happened." (Ibid.)

As its "lottery number" reveals, once again we have a case that gets more interesting the closer we look:

1. **A specially prepared and mounted surface for the purpose of reflecting images and viewing them,** (describes both projector screens and mirrors)
2. **falls,**
3. **in the dark,**
4. **creating a loud crash.**

Try to explain all *that* in terms of coincidence.

Jason himself, by the way, points out the importance of that first correlation:

> "I was also always intrigued by the almost metaphoric use of the (closed) projector screen in my dream, relating to my mirror (with no one looking at it at that moment) in reality. Or perhaps I'm reaching there!" (Ibid.)

No Jason, I don't think you are. Out of a virtually infinite range of possibilities, you chose to dream of a projector screen. But since you didn't know what was creating the ruckus, why did your sleeping self pick something that so closely resembles a mirror?

The skeptic's likely rebuttal would be that Jason could tell from the mere sound of the crash that it was indeed a mirror that fell, and his dreaming about a screen is therefore not surprising. But James emphatically denies that, so to take such a stance is to refute the only witness we have.

So here we have a lead-up dream in which the precise nature of the predicted event remains unknown (except for its sound) until *after* the dream has ended. And in terms of providing evidence for psi, that makes all the difference.

So once again: are lead-up dreams precognitive?

The notion that dreams that seem to go on for a long time are actually over in a flash, is a *hypothesis*. And as far as I can see, dream theorists favor it largely because it supports their assumption that psychic ability is an illusion.

But dreams certainly give the impression of taking place over an extended period. Not only does it feel that way to the dreamer, it looks that way to an outside observer. Anyone who watches someone writhing and moaning in the throes of a nightmare, or studies a subject's rapid eye movements (REM) over a period of many minutes, will find it hard to conclude that dreams run their course in an instant.

And remember: even if lead-up dreams last seconds, non-psi explanations don't work. Unless Maury's epic dream occurred entirely during the *milliseconds* between the rod hitting his neck and his waking up, how do we avoid seeing precognition at work?

("Milliseconds" is admittedly a guess. You can decide for yourself how long it would take for one to awaken in a situation like that.)

But let's say the skeptics are right, and a dream like Maury's, despite seeming to go on for ages, actually takes place in the blink of an eye. What does that say about dreams and time?

Here's what I see: whether they're precognitive or merely(!) proof of a nearly timeless mode of existence, lead-up dreams prove conclusively that during sleep, we can step outside time as we know it, and function in a way that seems impossible—even miraculous—to our waking selves.

Clearly, that's more than slightly suggestive of the case I'm making in this book.

It's possible, by the way, that depending on their precise timing, some of these lead-up-type cases are precognitive and some not. Despite our desire to fit all similar experiences into a single category, perhaps some of these dreams are about the past—if only by a fraction of a second—and others the future.

After all, nature doesn't create dreams with the intention of illustrating clear-cut categories.

But let's put aside the paranormal aspect for a moment, and focus on a simple, undeniable, fact:

At the heart of a lead-up dream is a double-entendre.

Two chapters ago I said that puns would play an important role in our story. In the case we were then discussing, the concept of "student loan" ended up being interpreted in two very different ways. And a dual meaning is the basis of a certain kind of pun, right?

In this chapter, we see the same dynamic. But rather than employing words or concepts, these double-entendres involve sensations or sounds. Whether it's the feeling of a metal rod hitting one's neck, a slight itch caused by an insect, or the noise created by a falling object, each of these seemingly predicted stimuli takes on two different meanings, one provided by the dream, and one by the waking event.

The double-entendres in lead-up dreams can also be visual, at least in part. A projector screen, when set up, looks much like a mirror. Not to mention that in James' dream, both were in the dark.

Here's a multimedia pun that incorporates imagery, sound, and language. S.M. Kovalinsky writes about an experience she had while sleeping in a hotel room:

> "I had a dream on Cape Cod, that I was driving with my husband, and the car broke down; [later] we sat in a shed with door slightly ajar; a cop pulled

up and asked, "Is there anyone in here?"

I awakened to a hotel assistant manager poking his head in the room, and asking that question--as though THAT fact were the cause of the dream." (Kovalinsky, 2008)

The correlations:

1. **The dreamer is at rest in a room away from home.**
2. **An authority figure . . .**
3. **looks through the doorway**
4. **and asks: "Is there anyone in here?"**

As you can see, the double-entendre is indeed complex, both verbal and visual.

Note, too, that in discussing puns, we're really re-visiting metaphors, because both are creative pairings of two things that are different, but which share one or more features.

This case is similar to James' in that the waking event was largely unknowable until *after* the dream was over. To avoid seeing precognition at work, you would need to argue that in the microscopic interval between hearing "Is anyone here?" and waking up, she determined that the speaker was standing in the doorway, and instantly dreamed the parallel scenario.

But remember, Ms. Kovalinsky was in a hotel, so the layout of the room would have been far from second nature to her.

And I don't know about you, but as I sleep, even in my own bed, I never seem to know where my physical body is actually located, as proven by the fact that when I awaken, unless I open my eyes immediately, it takes a while to grasp what part of the *country* I'm in, much less what house, room, and position within the room I'm occupying at that moment.

So when Ms. Kovalinsky heard those words while sleeping, how did her dreaming self know right away they were coming from someone standing in the doorway? And without that *instantaneous* knowledge, how and why did she dream up a convincing parallel scenario?

But, as I've been suggesting, even if this dream and the one about the falling projector screen didn't make it nearly impossible to avoid seeing precognition at work in at least some lead-up dreams, I would find them—and LUD's in general—invaluable. And that's because of their striking puns.

And if you're still asking yourself:

Why is this man making such a big deal of double-entendres?

I'll be delighted to answer that. In a book about proving the seemingly impossible, I've been careful to avoid presenting evidence that's either ambiguous or hard to substantiate. So when I suggest that you keep an eye out for puns, of all things, you might think I've lost my way.

But tell me—is there anything subtle about the guillotine double-entendre?

And whether or not precognition is involved, is there any doubt that Ms. Kovalinski dreamed about a cop asking a question through a doorway because that whimsically mirrored the real-life situation?

And I could ask a similar question about the mirror/projector screen dream.

In all three cases, the answer is obvious. And that's the point—LUD's prove that some dreams (a) not only feature double-entendres; and (b) not only are those puns unmistakable; but (c) the dream narratives exist for no other apparent reason.

Bottom line: lead-up dreams make it much harder to brush aside metaphors and puns in *all* cases in which they appear.

This stuff is real, folks.

A full definition.

In researching lead-up dreams, I was surprised to discover that despite their comprising a distinct, well-known, and utterly fascinating category unto themselves, no one seems to have bothered to give the phenomenon a name. As of this writing, if you Google "lead-up dream," you won't find it.

With that in mind, here's my definition:

A lead-up dream is one whose narrative leads up to, and provides an imagi-

nary explanation for, a real-world stimulus that awakens the dreamer. The waking event thus has one meaning in the dream, and another in reality. The double-entendre can involve sound, sensation, words, concepts, imagery, or any combination.

For example: a man enjoys a romantic dream leading up to and including a kiss, only to be awakened at the climactic moment by a dog licking his face.

(I wouldn't be surprised if some lead-up dreams involve the sense of smell, too.)

17. Two Leadup-Like Dreams (*The Honey-Trap Mystery, Bowling And Reincarnation*)

For me, a clear sign that at least some lead-up dreams are precognitive is their resemblance to a type of experience that pops up often in my experiment. What distinguishes cases of this sort from conventional LUD's is timing: dream and event don't overlap, and in terms of proving psi, that makes all the difference.

Think of it this way: what if Maury had awakened for no apparent reason, eyes closed, and only then, a second or two *after* the dream ended, fell victim to the canopy falling on his neck? Then the skeptic can no longer say Maury had the dream as a result of a sensation he was already feeling.

We could call such cases delayed-resolution LUD's, or leadup-*like* dreams. In this chapter we'll look at two. Featuring puns of the sort we've come to expect, they show, once again, that while fast asleep, we're not only psychic, but witty.

One sweet case.

One morning I woke up from the following strange and somewhat nonsensical dream. (Transcript condensed and slightly re-ordered for clarity):

"I'm part of a family . . . we're getting the answer to . . . a mystery that has long kept us puzzled.

It turns out that when we originally moved to our house, we . . . over-saturated the earth with honey. And that explains why you had a certain amazingly abundant growth of some plant over the years . . . we eat this plant and the plant. . . has a high honey content.

> *Now, we're learning . . . the dangers of over-consuming this plant . . . some person is educating us specifically as to the problems we're gonna face over the years as we consume . . . this honey-filled plant . . ."*

Now I shared this dream with a friend who said, essentially, "Honey? A health hazard?" Well, besides the fact that over-consumption of sugar (honey is 82% sugar) is a legitimate source of concern in 21st-century diets, I should explain that for me, the dream is particularly relevant. And I know I'm not alone.

You see, for many of us, a susceptibility to a certain fungus (candida) makes us especially sensitive to sugar in all its forms. And since I hardly need point out that sweets are addictive, maintaining a healthy diet under these circumstances can be tricky. So if my family has inadvertently caused there to be a veritable jungle of honey-filled plants ripe for the picking in our yard, and if that irresistible treat serves as a constant temptation—well, you get the idea.

OK. About four minutes later (effectively, that is, as I'll explain shortly), after checking for emails, finding none, and then glancing at the day's headlines, I'm reading a New York Times online review entitled " 'The Tall Blond Man With One Black Shoe': Cloak and Dagger and Farce." Roughly three minutes into reading the article, I see this (the bolding is mine):

> *François lurches from the concert hall into a **honey-trap**, with Mireille Darc . . . serving as expertly accommodating bait.* (Hoberman, 2015)

It's taken me a while, as always, to truly "get" this case (proof either of my idiocy, or the effort required to fully appreciate our dreams.) After being certain I had captured every last shred of evidence, the chapter underwent major revisions as additional points became clear—*twice.*

At first, all I knew was that it seemed at least slightly interesting that "honey"—a word I had just spoken 22 times while recording the dream minutes earlier—would show up in the very first thing I read (after glancing at a few headlines), and in a context that was guaranteed to make me sit up and take notice (the expression was new to me and the context erotic).

Only after thinking about the matter for a while did it occur to me: the dream is as much about a honey-*trap* as the movie scene! I mean, re-read that third paragraph in the dream excerpts above: given my special dilemma with sweets, could there be a better title for the dream scenario than "honey trap"?

Actually, the answer is yes. Because, as is now clear to me, to fully define the dream, we need to include all these:

1. In the context of a mystery (The full transcript repeats that word no less than three times.)

2. a honey trap

3. may do harm to the unaware.

OK. (Cue the drum-roll.) Since the NYT review describes the movie as "cloak-and-dagger," aren't *all three* also perfectly applicable to the sentence that constitutes the waking event?

(If you think I'm milking this case by adding a redundant or unnecessary correlation or two, the appendix discusses a movie scene I saw about five months later that, while referencing a honey trap, fails to meet the other criteria.)

Bullets and guns.

So the list of correlations is short, but odd and precise. As with Maury's guillotine dream, this case presents us with a pun that is unmistakable. Instead of involving a rap on the neck, the double-entendre here involves dual interpretations of the complete thought: "In the context of a mystery, a honey trap may do harm to the unaware."

Combined with the fact that, in practical terms, the dream came true nearly as quickly as Maury's—namely, almost right away—that spectacular pun tells us, beyond all reasonable doubt, that something meaningful is going on.

Here's another way to think about this: I think it's safe to say that this was the first time I ever had a dream that combined all three of the elements I just listed. Likewise, to the best of my knowledge, reading the article was the first time I encountered such a situation in real life. After spending about 25,000 days on this planet (69 years), what are the odds of those two firsts happening not just on the same day, but within *minutes* of each other?

We're back to those two colliding bullets—the sort of thing that happens (all together now): Every. Fourth. Dream. (At least, in my experiment.)

So, returning to the main point of this chapter:

Do you see the significance of leadup-*like* dreams such as this one?

I have a dream about a honey-trap within a mystery, then wake up to something that can be described in exactly the same terms. In this case, though, the real-world experience begins only after the dream has ended. So here, we can ignore the caveat that needs to be applied to conventional LUD's, since no one can say that the waking event influenced the dream, except paranormally.

To clarify the timing: remember our discussion two chapters ago about what I call the events pool? This case provides yet another example of the importance of the insights we gleaned there. The actual interval between recording the dream and seeing the word "honey-trap" was 37 minutes. But since most of that time was spent getting out of bed, going to the bathroom, and exercising in my living room (with no radio or TV in the background), the interim was *effectively* only about seven minutes—the time I spent online.

It was only during those seven minutes that I truly had a shot at finding correlations, so it would be statistically unfair to consider the pool of potential matching events to be larger.

It was small indeed.

(Full text and additional points in the Appendix.)

Bowling and Reincarnation.

Though strange and even a bit macabre, this next dream left me with a good feeling on awakening. Unlike *Honey Trap*, whose double-entendre can be expressed in a single sentence, this case involves several separate metaphors or puns, and some are visual.

Note that the all-important interim between recording and waking event is only about *five minutes*—and in this instance, not just effectively, but actually.

What happened is that one morning, right after waking up from a dream and documenting it, I went to the next room, opened my laptop, and almost immediately saw an email from a favorite author (Martha Beck) with this photo:

© Martha Beck 2015

And here are the correlations, along with quotes from the transcript. Note that I put myself in the shoes of the woman with the valise—an understandable substitution since the ad encourages readers to do exactly that.

"We're engaged in an activity that has some resemblance to bowling [spoken with an inflection that indicates surprise]. Certainly not that it is bowling."

A visual pun. Given the woman's posture and her position in relation to the lane, if the valise were a ball, wouldn't she look almost exactly like someone about to bowl? (My surprise shows how strange it is for me to have a dream about bowling.)

"You're facing towards what's almost like a single lane in a bowling alley . . . to each side of this 'lane' there's nothing whatsoever like another lane."

As you can see, the lane she faces is not surrounded by other lanes (as would be the case in a bowling alley).

"This is a constructive activity that requires courage."

A good match for a life-changing seminar entitled "The Quest."

"there seems like such a strong spiritual truth in this dream."

At the bottom, the ad speaks of "spiritual solutions."

"there's only a couple of people present with me . . . participating in this activity"

Just two people appear with the "bowler."

". . . the others seem to be able to do this . . . Someone says '. . . don't worry about this.' "

As predicted, the others in the scene are helpful and more experienced.

"you somehow hurl yourself down this lane"

Though "hurl" is not exactly the right word, the woman is indeed setting herself in motion down the lane.

"When you hit this blade headfirst, you die."

Another odd and precise visual pun. The "blade" is the light stripe that spans the upper part of the image, containing the date of the seminar. As predicted, the woman looks as if she's about to hit it headfirst.

"The blade is . . . almost like a single blade on a helicopter but it's spinning in a vertical plane rather than a horizontal plane. I'm not even sure that it's spinning but maybe it is."

If the "blade" in the photo were spinning, it would indeed spin in a vertical plane (like an airplane propeller).

" . . . 'death' is not accurate here since reincarnation is understood."

Deepak Chopra (on the left) is a renowned expert on reincarnation and related matters.

"Maybe I need to say good-bye to my friends before I do this . . . maybe that's what's holding me back."

The valise, the journey, and "Creating a Life You Love"—all imply a moving on with one's life.

"I'm wondering whether I have the courage to do this"

Whether or not to go ahead with this life-altering activity is the main question facing the reader.

Summing it up.

Once again, like Maury with his epic guillotine fantasy, I woke up from an elaborate dream, only to discover that it was a preview of, or variation on, something I would soon experience in the real world.

In my case, the "something" is: a spiritual activity that in certain ways resembles bowling, involves moving down a lane and striking a blade headfirst, and so on. As with *Honey Trap*, since the brief delay between dream and event makes this a leadup-*like* case, no one can say that my dreaming self was tipped off as to what was about to happen. (Because of its pun-like parallels and the fact that it came true in just 11 minutes, *Student Loan* probably also belongs in this category.)

Keeping in mind the tiny 5-minute interim, if psi weren't real, is this the sort of synchronicity you would expect to encounter in one out of four documented dreams?

And finally, if you agree that the dreams in this chapter seem genuinely precognitive, wouldn't that make it even more likely that the same is true for at least some *conventional* lead-up dreams, which they so closely resemble?

(More on this case in the Appendix.)

18. A Control Experiment

1994 saw my project enter its second year. What had begun in January of '93 with a single dream—the first I was willing to acknowledge as possibly precognitive—was gradually becoming a steady stream of such experiences. Many were hard to dismiss.

But to accept the reality of psi in my life wasn't easy. After so many years spent ridiculing all things psychic, fully trusting what my eyes were telling me would take time, and an important step along the way involved testing one of the last remaining conventional hypotheses I could think of.

Specifically, I had begun to wonder if it might be easier than I had been assuming to link dreams with waking events in a seemingly convincing fashion. A related possibility was that perhaps I had a rare gift for inventing meaningless correlations. Either of those scenarios appeared likelier to my inner skeptic than the idea I might be psychic.

I needed to discover the truth of the matter, so here's what I did.

An experiment within an experiment.

Without touching any of the other variables, I decided to eliminate psi from the equation. Would I still end up with one in four matches?

Omitting the psychic factor while leaving the others in place is more straightforward than you might think, and it can be accomplished, I believe, to a reasonable standard of reliability. After all, 87% of my precognitive dreams (as of this writing) came true within 24 hours, and only one took longer than 7 days. So in terms of my experiment, psi is largely irrelevant after a week.

With that in mind, I devised the following plan. On a given morning, at least two weeks after having a proven precognitive dream, I would wake up and pretend that I had the dream *that* morning instead of weeks earlier. I would then proceed, as with any newly-recorded dream, to see how it matched up with the day's upcoming events.

If random chance were the true explanation for these cases, wouldn't I be just as likely to find a match for the dream the second time around as the first? Not that I necessarily *would* find a second match, but assuming that I put in the same effort, the odds of doing so should be the same, right?

You understand, I wasn't expecting the same events to magically reoccur. But if my seemingly psychic dreams were merely the products of coincidence, then other experiences coming down the pike should match the dreams just as well.

I knew that a meaningful trial would depend on my daily routine remaining pretty much the same—visiting the same websites, watching a comparable amount of TV, etc. And for this experimenter, that was no problem—if ever there's someone who loves the easy, regular, repetition of certain favorite activities, that would be me.

So in May of '94 I carefully selected seven dreams, each of which had come true between two and three weeks earlier (except for one, which I now see was only a few days old, still largely beyond the likely influence of psi), and none of whose matching events had an obvious connection to a specific time-frame. Like the Times article with the honey-trap, the waking experiences in these seven cases seemed as likely to occur on day X, as on day Y.

(Obviously there were reasons the events happened when they did. But I had no way of knowing them, and that's the point.)

For an entire week, I started each day by going over the transcripts for all seven dreams. Remembering their details was easy, because they were recent cases to which I had given a great deal of thought. Their proximity in time also meant that my life's circumstances and routines hadn't changed much.

The results.

By the end of the week, I had logged 49 opportunities for dreams to come true (7 dreams multiplied by 7 days). 48 of those chances did not result in a match, and 1 did. (We'll talk about that one exception shortly.)

That's significant. According to my usual success rate, 49 dream-chances should result in about 12 instances of precognition (49 divided by 4). So my hit rate amounted to a twelfth of what I normally see.

But maybe you're thinking, "Now be honest, Bruce. Did you put as much effort into finding correlations as you usually do? You obviously give a great deal of thought to uncovering parallels when they work in favor of precognition. Are you sure you tried just as hard during the control experiment?"

I'm glad you asked. Because in one crucial respect I do *not* routinely work hard at this project at all. Specifically, I do not disrupt my normal activities by pondering a dream after recording it. That is, not until something happens that brings it to mind.

Think of the student loan case. On visiting the New York Times site, I clicked on an article that gave me not the slightest reason to think it might bear a relation to the dream I had just documented. And while reading it, I was fully involved in absorbing its content. Since my dreams are triggered by how I *feel* about an event, it's that whole-hearted engagement that makes precognition possible.

But when I saw "Who is Hillary Clinton to lecture me about repaying student loans?"—well, is it any surprise that at that point I stopped reading, thought about the dream, and the "work" of adding up possible correlations began?

There are exceptions to this. If a dream hasn't come true within hours, I may occasionally bring it to mind intentionally, just to make sure I haven't let an obvious correlation go by. But that's about it.

So yes: I think I was just as conscientious about finding synchronicities during the control experiment, as I normally am.

And remember, since I was tracking the same seven dreams for seven days, the content of those dreams was perpetually at my fingertips and in my thoughts. If correlations had come up, it would have been hard to miss them.

As to that twice-matched dream . . .

It's possible that this second match is a coincidence, especially since the later event doesn't correlate as convincingly with the dream as the original.

But it's an open question. I've documented a number of cases in which a dream did in fact clearly foreshadow more than one upcoming experience. And given what we know about dreams, this shouldn't come as a surprise.

Remember I said that dreams of the future are identical to "routine" ones except for the one obvious difference? Well, few of us would doubt that a dream can incorporate data collected at various and sundry times in the *past*. For example, I might dream that someone I met for the first time yesterday is conversing with a childhood friend I haven't seen in ages.

So why not a dream that references tomorrow and also next week?

Here's another way to think about this. Consider the notorious I'm-back-in-school-and-unprepared-for-an-exam nightmare. I've noticed that while having such a dream, I'm always 100% convinced that it's about an actual experience. That's why the dream is so powerful—it feels real.

Then I wake up, ponder the dream, and realize it's not what it seemed. While the fear is genuine, the details can't be tied to a single historical event. The school, the people, and the test subject are all real enough, but the way the dream *combines* them proves it never actually happened.

Dreams, in other words, are often about *classes* of objects, people, experiences. We dream of watching a baseball game, let's say, and, while dreaming, are utterly certain of its authenticity and specificity. But the fact is, it may draw on many games we've seen, and be colored by our imagination as well.

So—whether it points towards yesterday or tomorrow, a dream can reference more than one experience in the physical world. And that may well have been the case with the lone example in my control test that came up with a second match. I've seen this in other instances too—cases in which I'm nearly certain that *both* matches are legitimate. Nevertheless, it remains a fact that a large majority of my precognitive dreams leave me with the clear impression that they predict just a single event.

Conclusion

I don't claim that my control experiment is perfect. But I will say this: anyone who tries it will discover that dreams are not as easily matched with real-life events— to the *same standards* I've been demonstrating in this book—as you might think.

And that's the point.

(Skeptics: I strongly encourage you to put the protocol I've described in this chapter to the test. Use any dream whatsoever—it doesn't have to have been part of a larger experiment. Just make sure to choose a dream that's a few weeks old, to lessen the chance you'll be uncovering actual evidence of precognition!)

PART 5: MINING YOUR DREAMS

19. Why These Dreams Matter

So maybe you're wondering, what's the point? Even if precognition is genuine, the sorts of dreams I've been sharing would hardly seem capable of making a difference in anyone's life.

But keep in mind that the purpose of my experiment is simply to find out if psi is real. I recorded the dreams in this book not because they seemed flush with useful information, but for their oddness and potential for being verified.

Now Derek's dream was both evidential *and* helpful. If I had similar, properly documented, experiences of my own to share I would, but as I've said, I'm not a particularly gifted psychic. Be that as it may, eminently practical instances of precognition are far from rare. Adopting the broadest of perspectives, Larry Dossey says: [POP p. xxii]

> For most of human history, foreknowledge has not been regarded as hypothetical, but as a natural part of the human endowment . . . Premodern cultures routinely used, and still use, premonitions pragmatically: Knowing where danger lay, where to find game and shelter, when to plant and harvest, where to locate strayed animals, or which part of which plant, harvested in which season, prepared in which way, would cure a specific illness. (Dossey, 2009)

Since success in such endeavors is critical for survival, it's not likely indigenous peoples would waste precious energy on superstition.

But familiarity with, and respect for, psi, is not restricted to cultures we call "primitive"—many doctors, therapists, and business people have discussed the importance of their psychic dreams in gaining information that has been indispensable in their work. And if you're wondering why we don't hear about these things more often, ask yourself: if a doctor who used his paranormal abilities came out of the closet, what would be the likelihood of his being embraced by the medical establishment? He might even scare off some of his patients.

In a later chapter I'll introduce you to books with case histories illustrating the sorts of benefits of precognition we've just been discussing. But for now, I'd like to shift the focus to what is for me more familiar territory. Because in my case, and I'll venture for many other people as well, the real gift involved in having such dreams is of a different kind entirely. And it has to do with . . .

Getting past what we've been told.

Perhaps you think that even if precognition is real, it's nothing to get excited about—just an unexplained oddity that will someday be proven perfectly compatible with the materialist paradigm. Give the old model a tweak or two and we can move on to more important matters.

But if that's your opinion, I wonder if you've thought things through. Could a desire to avoid cognitive dissonance be clouding your judgment? Because as I see it, the ramifications of dreams like mine are profound.

For one thing, they tell us that the universe in its entirety must be even more enormous than we thought. Or perhaps I should say more complex, since the notion of size—which implies physicality—may itself be a red herring.

Because if I can have a dream that reveals ordinarily unknowable facts about tomorrow, then tomorrow already exists. I don't see any way around this. How can I retrieve information from the future unless, in some way, it exists side-by-side with the present? (This is especially apparent with more robust dreams like Derek's in which not just bits and pieces of the future are seen in advance, but long, detailed, scenarios, plain as day.)

Furthermore, if science is dead wrong about something as significant as precognition, what else might it be missing? In particular, don't we now need to take a second look at other phenomena we've been sweeping under the rug with the label "paranormal"?

Obviously, we do. If something as seemingly outrageous as seeing the future is a fact of life, then the floodgates are open, and other non-materialistic claims can no longer be dismissed out of hand. As you may know, there are many phenomena for which parapsychology has been quietly amassing mountains of evidence, even as the more mainstream sciences have turned a blind eye—and for some of the same reasons, discussed earlier, that it discounts precognition.

Many of these phenomena are particularly suggestive with respect to one particular aspect of reality. It's the single lesson or upshot of psi that most directly affects us, the one with the greatest potential to alter our perspective on that most worrisome of questions: is death to be feared?

Beyond the body.

Consider this: if I have a dream in which I verifiably see or experience the future, doesn't that mean I'm somehow already *in* the future?

And though we've been focusing on the temporal aspects of these dreams, a similar insight applies if we view them spatially. I once had a dream that revealed details (later verified) of a law office I would soon visit for the first time. And much the same happened with both a campground and a park.

Doesn't that mean I somehow visited those locations as I slept? Or, as mind-boggling as it seems, that I'm always there?

And if I already exist in the future and at remote locations, or even if my dreaming self just paid a visit, then what part of me are we talking about, anyway? What is this "I" that seems to be everywhere and everywhen? It's not my body, obviously, because that's safely tucked in bed.

As I see it, it's inescapable: the reality of precognition means that we are more than our physical selves.

Putting this in context.

Now if you're wondering whether I'm saying that precognition proves we survive death, let me put it this way: I'm confident we do. And my dreams, in combination with other influences, have played an important role in convincing me.

In the final section of this book, I'll be more explicit as to how this change of heart and mind came about in my life. And we'll look at further grounds for thinking that my conclusions aren't as far-fetched as they might seem.

In the meantime, I'd like to end this chapter by sharing with you . . .

What a fellow dream explorer learned.

I used to hang out regularly at Alex Tsakiris' excellent Skeptiko forum. On a thread about precognitive dreams, a commenter named Jake Bailey (screen name: Soulatman) wrote the following:

> Putting a little effort into paying attention to my dreams was what finally gave me the evidence I needed that there just may be a soul (or something akin to that), or at least a deeper wisdom at work, and I was connecting with it while asleep.

> I had a significant number of precognitive dreams. These have permanently reoriented my perspective on reality, away from a materialist reductionist paradigm. In truth, I have no idea which scientific or philosophical model of reality is the most accurate. But it is so very nice to know that some models must be emphatically wrong as they can offer no explanation for my experiences, and indeed, are entirely falsified by them.

> A huge payoff, for such a little effort. The experience of precognitive dreaming has given me a confidence in and certainty about life's mystery and magic that materialist science will never again be able to threaten. (Bailey 2014)

And with that, I invite you to join Jake and me in one of the grandest adventures I know.

20. Do *You* Dream The Future?

While I can't prove it, I think it's likely we all have precognitive dreams. And by showing how the evidence escapes us, and how best to bring it to light, I'd like to usher this remarkable phenomenon into the mainstream. Not just as a point of information, but as firsthand experience.

Obviously, few readers will be as devoted to the subject as I am. That's fine. But like Jake, you may find that a fairly small effort yields significant rewards.

And if you have a hard time imagining that you yourself could harbor such an ability, then

Remember how surprised *I* was.

I can't overstate how amazed I was, back in the early 1990's, to discover evidence for precognition turning up in my dreams. I was in my mid-forties, remember, before I suspected such a thing was even possible, having long believed so-called psychic abilities were the biggest sham going. And the fact is, despite my experiences, my experiment, and the arguments I've been making in this book, there's a part of me that's still astonished each and every time a dream turns out to have an unexplainable connection to a future event.

Talk to your friends.

Here's a suggestion: if you're interested in testing—and maybe even moving beyond—your skepticism, sound out the people you know. When I tried that myself back when I was just starting to be psi-curious, I was amazed at the number of friends and acquaintances who had had impressive psychic dreams they were happy to share. And I *grilled* these people. I made a nuisance of myself, asking them the same sorts of skeptical questions I keep raising in this book, floating one conventional explanation after another to see if I could somehow explain away what was so hard for me to accept.

But the universe was apparently intent on getting through to me, because I kept running into these closet psychics—even in situations where I didn't particularly expect to. Many were acquaintances with little or no interest in parapsychology: a neighbor and former piano student, a fellow teacher, a co-worker at a sales office where I worked—even my very conservative dentist.

Even friends who had good reason to *deny* such experiences were reporting them. Remember my neighbor Arthur, whom you read about earlier? As I mentioned, despite his obvious discomfort with the paranormal, he shared a whopper of a precognitive dream. As did Pierre, a therapist-in-training at the psi-denying therapy center that's played such an important role in my life. Pierre, in fact, surprised me by recounting *many* startling dreams—though I doubt he was telling his boss about them.

So ask around—you may be surprised at what happens next. One of the rewards of an interest in the paranormal is its way of opening unexpected areas, and depths, of communication. I find that often, with a little encouragement, friends, or even near-strangers, are delighted to discuss experiences they have found intriguing, and in many cases, life-changing.

Signs that you may already be experiencing precognition.

I hesitate to raise the following points, because in doing so I step outside the boundaries of my experiment. And that makes me vulnerable to the skeptic's usual objections—bias confirmation, the law of large numbers, wishful thinking, etc.

So let's just say I'd like to talk *possibilities* here. With that in mind, ask yourself if any of these ring a bell:

• **Casually dismissed "coincidences."** Once I began to take the possibility of precognition seriously, I remembered that there had been occasions in the past when conversations or other waking experiences would suddenly bring to mind dreams from the previous night. I now think it's likely that some of those dreams, with their odd and unexpected correlations to later events, were in fact, psychic.

● **Episodes of waking precognition.** While awake, do you ever have startlingly clear knowledge, beyond all explanation, of what will happen in the next few moments? Precognition is *not* restricted to the hours we spend sleeping.

● **Déjà vu**. While I myself have little or no personal experience with it, déjà vu is an obvious candidate for a mystery that may be explainable, at least sometimes, by precognitive dreams.

● **Pre-alarm wake-ups.** When I was much younger, my morning routine often involved waking up to the sound of a bedside radio, set to begin playing at a certain time. And I noticed a startling fact: time and again, I would awaken seconds *before* the radio turned itself on. In those days, remember, I was a randomaniac par excellence—odd synchronicities were the last things I was looking for or wanting to have happen.

But happen, they did—at least in this regard. While I can't recall all the specifics, I clearly remember my astonishment at the startling precision of the phenomenon, and its sheer frequency.

All these years later, having by now documented numerous instances of dreams that came true just moments after awakening, I'm inclined to think that those pre-alarm wake-ups weren't coincidental after all. I suspect they were the result of my dreaming self being kind to me, saving me from the indignity of a forced, mechanical, rousing from sleep.

And here's another point to ponder. Remember my skeptical neighbor Arthur? He tells me he's experienced this phenomenon himself, and that it doesn't seem explainable as the workings of some sort of biological clock. Because during the period of his life when he woke up to an alarm, he was surprised to see that regardless of what time he retired, arose, and how much sleep he got, the results would be the same.

● **Lead-up dreams.** I've had at least one, as I've said. How about you?

In sum, while none of these odd manifestations are guaranteed to be of paranormal origin, the walks-like-a-duck rule just may apply. So, if you're looking for a sign of latent psychic ability and have experienced one or more of the above, that sign may be there for the taking.

What does Darwin have to do with this?

By the time Darwin published *Origin of Species* he had amassed a great deal of evidence pointing to the truth of natural selection. Though common sense dictates he had been able to study only a tiny percentage of existing life forms, his data was so compelling, and his theory so adept at explaining the facts on the ground, he assumed that the principles of evolution must apply to all species. (I know—Darwin's contribution raises as many questions as it answers. But that doesn't negate its importance.)

I think an analogy is in order. It's not one I can prove, but it's my best guess.

The work of precognition hunters like myself, not to mention the countless experiences of ordinary dreamers throughout history, points unequivocally to the reality of the phenomenon. And I, for one, suspect that it's as universally applicable as evolution. If I'm the result of evolution, so are you. If I dream of the future, so do you.

Now some may say the situation is different. There's no way evolution could be at work in my life but not in yours, or in the ancestry of a fish but not that of a giraffe. But psychic ability? Even if it's a fact of life, there's no reason to think it's a trait we all share.

If that's your objection, and assuming you agree that precognition is real, think of it this way. We all dream, and we all dream of the past. Does it make sense that only *some* of us dream of the future?

21. How To Observe Precognition On Your Own

Remembering your dreams.

If you think you might enjoy exploring your dreams but can't remember any, J.W. Dunne has a suggestion: when you wake up, instead of trying to recall a dream, think back to your first conscious *thought*, because that will often take you back to what you were dreaming moments earlier.

You may find that re-living that first dream primes the pump, so to speak, allowing other dreams to come to mind.

At that point, you may be faced with a challenge of a different sort. When several dreams compete for your attention, it can be tricky to document all of them before they vanish. (The expression "like herding cats" comes to mind.)

One solution is to quickly jot down a few key reminders about each dream, then pick what seems to be the most promising dream, record it in detail, and quickly return to the others.

This strategy has its disadvantages, though. If the first dream takes a long time to record, you may forget important aspects of the others despite your notes. It's a dilemma without a perfect solution.

Deciding which dreams and visions to record.

If you're trying to prove the existence of psi, there's no point documenting dreams that don't have the potential to provide solid evidence. Giving some thought as to which dreams to record improves your chances of capturing that most coveted of all prizes in this experiment—the once-in-a-lifetime dream that predicts an equally unexpected event.

Even better, of course, is when that dream comes true instantly or nearly so, and I'll have some suggestions as to how to facilitate that.

With that in mind, here are some guidelines for dream selection.

Ignore recurring dreams.

I long ago stopped recording dreams with themes that re-appear night after night, and which introduce little in the way of fresh or unexpected elements.

For example, I often dream about the following: coming up to bat in a baseball game; being threatened by soldiers or criminals; seeing certain childhood friends; and being unprepared to play in an upcoming piano recital. If I have a dream involving one of those scenarios, and the next day something happens that seems to match it, my feeling is: "well, since I have that dream night after night, it was bound to come true sooner or later!"

Similarly, eliminate dreams that bring to mind routine waking events.

I tend to avoid dreams about music because I often spend a good chunk of my day playing the piano, teaching private students, composing, and so forth. Easily predictable events obviously make for less compelling matches.

On the other hand, if, in my dream, a student were to sit down at the piano, shout "hallelujah!" and proceed to play a Bach Fugue with her elbows . . . well, a scenario like that would certainly get me wondering what in the world might have caused me (or be *about* to cause me, as strange as that sounds) to conjure up such a thing.

In other words:

Go for the weird.

Don't ignore a dream just because it seems too strange to come true. If your dream life is anything like mine, those are precisely the sorts of scenarios that will often turn up in your waking reality—though perhaps in ways or contexts you would never have expected.

Avoid dreams that can be explained by recent past events.

Even if such a dream seemed to come true, you'd wonder if it had more to do with yesterday's event or today's.

Pay attention to dreams that have a certain power or intensity.

While I often find good evidence for precognition in dreams that might be described as low-key, some of my best cases involve dreams that are particularly vivid.

How to document a dream.

Above all, record your dreams without delay. On occasion, I've awakened in the middle of the night from a spectacular dream, marveled at it for a while, and then gone back to sleep, confident I'll remember it in the morning. Sadly, I never do (and other dream enthusiasts have described similar disappointments).

Also, I've learned that it's easier to capture a dream by narrating it onto my iPod than by writing it out. That's especially true when I've just awakened (as is always the case) and am still rubbing the sleep out of my eyes.

Actually, I use a combination approach: In addition to recording my dreams, I also keep index cards by my bed so that for each dream I choose to document, I can jot down a title, a sentence or two describing it, and maybe even dash off a simple drawing. (A little sketch can make a world of difference.)

Then I can refer to my notes during the day if I need a quick reminder of what I dreamt.

Be sure to document the date and time as you begin to record. And equally important, announce the time as you *finish*. Since the interval between dream and waking event can be helpful in determining the strength of the case, and since nothing of interest is likely to happen while making the recording, it's the *end* time that marks the start of the countdown to the real-world event. (Assuming, of course, that you woke up from the dream and began documenting it immediately.)

Capture as much detail as possible.

In general, the more specifics you record, the better. Focus on what's concrete and unquestionable within the dream, rather than what you assume *might* be the case, your interpretation of what *may* be happening, or speculation on how you think the dream might match up with a later event.

In other words: just the facts, ma'am.

Next step: live your life!

Having documented one or more *provable* dreams (as discussed), you've laid the groundwork and done it well. So at this point simply trust in the process, enjoy your day, and let the universe work its magic.

Note that being on the lookout for matching events doesn't require any special effort or thought. (Which would only be counterproductive by distancing you from the richness of your experience, a key impetus for psi.) That first clue is usually fairly obvious. A quick glance at the examples in this book shows that each was brought to my attention by something that, while typically not "hitting me over the head," did, in fact, spontaneously make me think of the dream.

Keep in mind too that a prime characteristic of my cases, as I've said, is that the predicted events are of considerable interest to me. By which I mean they're *intrinsically* interesting. Apart from the fact that I dreamt about it, that helicopter story on the late news was intriguing; the fallen limb blocked my path and created a problem I had to solve; *Round Object* involved a hypothetical scenario so strange and magical I felt compelled to put myself into the picture; and so on. This is one of many factors that demonstrate the logic and consistency of the phenomenon.

So if you want to observe precognition, fill your hours with activities that are fresh and engaging. That's the best way to increase the likelihood that one of them will retroactively trigger a dream (as bizarre as that sequence of events sounds).

And remember that anything you do to try to *make* a specific dream come true obviously undermines the integrity of your results. The rule is simple: live your life as if you were not conducting an experiment. With one exception, perhaps: during the day, you might wish to glance occasionally at your dream notes to see if you may have already experienced a predicted event. I didn't realize that one of my more intriguing dreams was precognitive until the next *day*, though that's a rarity. Almost always, I'll become aware that a matching event is unfolding in real time.

Finally, here's a biggie: be alert to what happens soon—often immediately—after waking up from a dream. We've explored several cases from my files in which dreams came true in minutes (either actually, or effectively), and I've seen this happen on many other occasions as well (though sometimes without proper documentation).

I'll say it again: 39% of my dreams came true within an hour.

A variation: use pre-selected targets.

You might take advantage of the immediacy factor by preparing a target you can look at right after awakening. (Or right after meditating, as I'll discuss in a moment.) On several occasions, before going to sleep, I set up my bedside laptop in such a way that the first thing I would see in the morning on lifting the lid, would be a photo or illustration on a website that serves up random images. (Google "random image generator.")

It took some fiddling to figure out how to accomplish this without accidentally glancing at the image beforehand, but it can be done.

Another possibility is to blindly slip a bookmark into a magazine with lots of pictures, or ask a friend to do that for you.

Though I got some intriguing results on several occasions using such methods, I haven't chosen to go this route very often. For me, part of the fun is seeing how precognition manifests spontaneously—what sort of events my sleeping self picks up on as I simply go about living my life, doing what I like to do.

But you might want to take that last remark with a grain of salt. The books by Upton Sinclair and Dale Graff in the Resources Chapter describe in detail how these authors carried out their own impressive experiments using pre-selected image targets. Graff's chapter is especially relevant since he was specifically working with precognition.

Why meditation may be your best ally as you look for psi.

I said earlier in the book that some of my cases involve visions that came to me while meditating, and I explained why I treat them as if they were dreams. Two examples are *Round Object* and *Student Loan*. (The latter is a borderline situation because I fell asleep while meditating.)

What I haven't mentioned is my remarkable success rate with these visions. Out of the eight I documented, five ended up as 2's (proven cases), one was a 1 (a maybe), and only two were 0's (no sign of precognition).

I think these surprising results are due to the fact that while meditating, I'm in a peaceful state that makes it easier to align with that part of me that resides outside time and space. (Note that the sort of meditation I practice has nothing to do with thinking, but is characterized, rather, by the *absence* of thought. Its focus is on relaxing, letting go of routine activities and concerns, and communing with what I think of as my larger self.)

And because I'm alert and focused *after* meditating, whatever I encounter at that point is likely to capture my undivided attention, leading to the sort of vivid experience that triggers these visions—and what's more, leading to it quickly. (Three of my visions resulted in nearly instant matches.)

You might even consider using meditation in conjunction with the random image strategy—just set up a target beforehand that you can look at as you emerge from your peaceful respite.

And lest you forget a point driven home by several of my cases: if something happens during the day that you suspect may be linked to last night's dream . . .

Don't be thrown off the scent by unexpected lead actors.

We've seen how precognitive dreams can mask their psychic connection to real-life experiences by altering certain aspects of the events. Especially common are changes in protagonist. For example, you may find that your dreams substitute one gender for the other, or insert you, the dreamer, into the plot.

An example of gender switching is *Student Loan*, in which Hillary Clinton took Mr. Plumley's place. Note, though, that what *hasn't* changed is significant: like Mr. Plumley, Clinton is the older and more experienced of the two characters, and in keeping with the story line, she is the "teacher" and a member of the same profession.

Student Loan, *Round Object*, *Bowling*, and *Honey Trap*, are examples of dreams in which real-life participants are replaced by the dreamer himself—in this case, me. In each, it's easy to grasp the logic behind that substitution: In *Student Loan*, I am, appropriately, the less experienced colleague (compared to Mr. Plumley) and student; with *Round Object* and *Bowling*, the dream is a result of my later *picturing* myself as the protagonist—the *Bowling* ad, indeed, clearly encourages its readers to do exactly that.

Finally, in *Honey Trap*, my real-life struggle with sugar makes me an obvious candidate for a leading role in a story about the danger of being "trapped" by honey.

Fully document the waking event, too.

As suspected matching events unfold, keep track of what you're experiencing in the moment, preferably by recording it immediately. For example, if you misunderstand an article you're reading, your dream may well have captured your initial error, rather than the true intent of the piece. So it's important to document such details while they're fresh.

Make a list of correlations.

While weighing the evidence is the subject of the *next* chapter, the process begins, in truth, as soon as the first clues appear. Because right from the start you're asking yourself, "Is this precognition?" You want to know, understandably, if the incident is worth pursuing, and that calls for a preliminary evaluation.

So this is where a list of correlations comes into play. Here again, for example, is the one I drew up for *Student Loan*:

1. **A long-term loan to a student,**
2. **the need for which has essentially ended,**
3. **is the cause of a conflict between two people in the same field.**
4. **One is older, more experienced, and acts as teacher.**
5. **The younger is the student and borrower.**
6. **The disagreement has been triggered by the older person's stance on**

the return of the borrowed item.

7. **The situation is reported to us directly by the younger person,**

8. **who expresses his annoyance.**

We've talked in detail about these parallels, so I won't say much about them now. The key is to look for whatever similarities you can find, be they literal or approximate.

For hits that are approximate, word them in such a way that they are *literally true for both dream and waking event*. This isn't about *changing* anything, of course—it's about finding legitimate common ground.

For example, correlation #1 involves two different kinds of loans—but long-term loans nevertheless. In #3, "the same field" refers to music in the dream, and politics in the waking event. And in #4, while Clinton is not really a teacher, Rubio is mad at her for lecturing him, so "teacher" is clearly applicable.

And if you think this is mere trickery—that I'm playing up random similarities that have no real meaning—then try the control experiment detailed in a previous chapter. Choose any dreams you like, and see if you can match them up to today's waking events as convincingly as I've done in the cases presented in this book. (I say *today's* events because the vast majority of my precognitive dreams came true the same day, and several within minutes.)

Of course, if you *can* come up with equally persuasive cases, you just may be seeing psi at work!

So the question then becomes: how can we know? How can we determine if the impossible is actually happening?

That's what we'll talk about next.

22. Evaluating The Evidence

D on't be discouraged if it takes a while to uncover your first precognitive dream. Keep in mind that although you may end up with a smaller percentage of successes than I, it's equally possible that your best cases, taken individually, will be more impressive.

Besides, as I hope you'll agree based on the examples I've been sharing, for psi to be proven it wouldn't be necessary for a quarter of our dreams to come true. Even if the fraction were much smaller, precognition would still be impossible to explain away.

In any case, as you begin to experiment, remember that a large majority of my dreams (and probably yours) are *not* psychic.

For example, just yesterday I woke up from a dream that startled me. Because of its vividness and its quality of seeming utterly out of place in the context of my life, it reminded me of some of my best cases.

But it didn't pan out. Nothing happened over the next twenty-four hours to bring the dream to mind. So unless it turns out to be among the small percentage of my dreams that takes more than a day to come true, this is one of the 75% that's not precognitive.

Did I waste a lot of time on it? Hardly. Though I did put some effort into recording the dream, the time I spent looking for a match was minimal. Just a few minutes in total, as I occasionally reflected on the dream during the day, while mentally scanning recent events looking for similarities.

As I've said, the bulk of the detective work begins *after* something happens that brings the dream to mind.

So let's talk about that. Let's say that at this very moment you're experiencing the odd, magical, mysterious feeling of seeing or doing something that makes you think: wow, that's a bit like the dream I just had. Could my dream really have predicted this?

What to look for.

All along we've been discussing the strengths and weaknesses of the cases I've been sharing. So by now you should have a pretty good idea of how to evaluate your own dreams as evidence for psi; consider what follows as a handy checklist of the key points, with some additional insights added to the mix.

First, here's the whole list without explanation. I'm assuming your dream is properly documented so accuracy of memory isn't an issue, and that you've already made a list of possible correlations, as described in the previous chapter.

1. **How odd is the dream?**
2. **How odd is the waking event?**
3. **How plentiful and precise are the correlations?**
4. **How long did it take for the dream to come true?**
5. **How likely is it that you could have known about the matching event through non-psychic means?**

I consider those the main points; here are two more:

6. **From your perspective, how interesting or engaging was the waking event?**
7. **Was the main thrust of the waking event similar to the main thrust of the dream?**

Now let's look at the criteria one at a time. As I've said, the first two should be weighed immediately *on awakening* from a dream, since there's little point in even bothering to document routine dreams about routine events. And keep in mind that even though a case may be relatively unimpressive in certain respects, unusual strength in other areas may balance that out.

1. How odd is the dream?

Often, only the dreamer can answer this with certainty. Think about it: for all you know, I'm an aeronautics fanatic who dreams about helicopter stunts nightly, making the first example in this book less impressive.

But of course, that's not the case. The dream was a radical departure from my usual ones, and that's half the formula that defines compelling cases like *Spinning Blades*, in which a once-in-a-lifetime dream is quickly replicated by a once-in-a-lifetime experience.

Which brings us to the next point:

2. How odd is the waking event?

Again, the answer depends on who's doing the experimenting—an unusual occurrence in the context of my life might be routine for you, and vice-versa.

3. How plentiful and precise are the correlations?

This, of course, is two separate questions combined into one, and both need to be taken into consideration. Take *Student Loan* and *Bowling and Reincarnation*, for example. The fact that most of the hits are metaphoric is less than a selling point.

On the other hand, the sheer *number* of hits in each case is impressive. And just as important is how they measure up to the following test:

4. How long did it take for the dream to come true?

Student Loan found its match in my first experience (for our purposes) following the dream. In other words, what we've been calling the pool of potential matching events was virtually empty. Except, that is, for one thing—my reading the review that contained the bulls-eye. (The targeted quote shows up about three minutes into the article, making the entire interim 11 minutes or less.)

Much the same is true for *Bowling and Reincarnation,* and in both cases, this immediacy, together with the large number of hits, makes up for the symbolic nature of the correlations.

Remember, in determining the length of the interval between dream and waking event, the time you spend recording the dream doesn't count, since nothing is likely to happen during that time that might generate a provable precognitive dream.

5. How likely is it that you could have known about the matching event through non-psychic means?

This is often dependent on the answer to question #2 because if the matching event is unusual, it's generally less likely that you would have known about it in advance. But that's not always the case—something can be rare but nevertheless expected (eclipses and approaching hurricanes, for example).

And then, our two less crucial tests:

6. From your perspective, how interesting or engaging was the waking event?

An experience that evokes an emotional response would seem more likely to trigger a dream than a bland one, so a matching event that's especially meaningful is a plus factor.

On days my inner skeptic is insistent, I remind myself that the waking events in my cases are almost always attention-grabbers in their own right, quite apart from their links to dreams. Sometimes they'll coincide with one of the day's high (or low) points.

These cases are organic, and make good, intuitive, sense. They *feel* real.

7. Does the dream correlate, in its *entirety*, to the waking event?

In each of the cases I've presented, the *bulk* of the dream corresponds with the real-life experience. I'm not cherry-picking one small corner of the dream—I'm taking into consideration the whole thing, as the complete transcripts in the appendices show.

(As you digest that, bear in mind a related point: what I've been calling "matching events" vary enormously in size or duration. In *Honey Trap*, for example, the matching event is largely confined to my reading the sentence containing the phrase "honey trap," though the title, with its "cloak-and-dagger" reference, also figures in. If this seems arbitrary, it simply reflects what a precognitive dream does—it captures a piece of the future, large or small.)

But there's a caveat: a case can fail miserably in meeting this criterion while still offering compelling proof of psi. If you've forgotten how and why, please take another look at the chapter called *The Lottery Number Concept*.

Balancing strengths and weaknesses.

In evaluating a case, a relative weakness may be offset by strengths in other areas. (Though if you had some non-psychic way of knowing about the event in advance, that's obviously a flaw beyond redemption.) Several cases in this book illustrate this point, as I'll now explain.

We've talked about how, helping to account for our ignorance of our psychic ability, is that the evidence is sometimes metaphoric: something within the dream *resembles* a key aspect of a later waking experience, rather than precisely duplicating it.

All things being equal, and for obvious reasons, metaphoric hits are weaker than literal ones. But each case needs to be judged *as a whole*. Which is why your list is so important. By re-stating approximations and turning them into literal parallels, as discussed, you make them more conducive to objective evaluation. Put enough of those "softer" correlations together, and, especially if the dream comes true quickly, you may have a winning-lottery-number effect that's hard to ignore.

And that's precisely the situation with what I've been calling my leadup-like cases: *Student Loan, Honey Trap,* and *Bowling and Reincarnation*.

Putting it all together.

Having arrived at this stage, like a juror at a criminal trial, you will likely have come to some conclusion as to the strength of the case. And the legal analogy is a good one: in this experiment, as in our judicial system, there are no mathematical formulas on which we can rely. All one can do is examine the evidence, ponder all points of view, and decide.

Now some will say that's not good enough—important matters like the validity of psi should rest on clearly defined calculations. But the fact is, what I've just described is not only how we make life-or-death decisions in the courtroom, it's how we arrive at all our most important understandings. When it comes to what really matters to us—relationships, health, finances, and so on—though science may offer support, we're largely on our own.

Maybe questions about psi and the spiritual dimension need to be added to that list.

Having said that, if you're like me, you will want to bring as much logic and objectivity to this experiment as possible. And for that reason, you might want to score your dreams and calculate your success rate, perhaps using the approach I detailed at the end of the chapter called *Methods and Definitions*.

As I've said, what matters more than individual cases may be the overall pattern. For me, that's what turned an intriguing "maybe" into a "no doubt about it."

On the other hand, if you were to have only one precognitive dream in your entire life, and if it were *extremely* compelling, that single experience might be all it would take—for *you*.

What to expect as you begin.

If you agree that the cases I've shared provide solid evidence of precognition, then keep in mind that few, if any, had me convinced from the start. Except for *Spinning Blades* and *Fallen Limb*, the cases in this book merely hinted at the possibility that something out of the ordinary might be going on. That is, until I put all the clues together.

If I've stressed this point repeatedly, it's because it's one of the most important to be made, and is true for the vast majority of my precognitive dreams: time and again I was amazed to see how a careful examination of *all* the relevant facts could transform a hunch into a clear knowing.

But this is to be expected, isn't it? For if the evidence hiding in our dreams were instantly persuasive, what would explain our missing it for so many years?

So record your dreams and be alert during the day. If something happens that brings a dream to mind for any reason, take note of what you're experiencing, and review your documentation of the dream's details. While there may be nothing at all to the matter, a closer look just may bring to light evidence with the power to forever change how you see yourself and your world.

PART 6: THE LARGER CONTEXT

23. Awakening to a Greater Reality—My Story

By providing first-hand proof of the spiritual dimension, my dreams radically changed me. And if ever there were a surprising turn of events, it was this. For if I had never been exactly a *militant* skeptic (since I didn't see myself as crusading for a cause), I was certainly an arrogant one.

But stumbling on evidence of my own psychic ability wasn't the only revelation chipping away at my defenses, softening me, leading me in a new direction. Nor was it the first. Other discoveries figured into the picture as well, and one was particularly important. As you'll see, it opened the door to all the rest.

To tell the story, I need to set the stage with some personal history.

The making of a skeptic.

Though comparing one's experience to that of others is a tricky business at best, I think it's fair to say that my childhood was unusually difficult. To put it bluntly, I received little of the loving support I would imagine most people take for granted.

Later, as a young adult grappling with the challenges that often arise from such a start, I was drawn to a form of psychotherapy that would become a dominant force in my life. While helping me, it also kept me focused, by virtue of its founder's philosophy, on a path that was atheistic and materialistic. (The latter, in the sense that matter is all that matters).

As I explained in Chapter 12, all during my long involvement with this therapy—a full twenty years—not only didn't I believe in psychic phenomena, the mere mention of the subject made me angry. It was in conflict, you see, with what I held to be The One Truth. For what should have been strictly a therapy had become, as a result of how I approached it, a religion.

But after all those years in therapy, though I had come a long way, my life was still a struggle, and I was depressed. And it was in this state of mind, in 1990, that I happened to sign up for a book club. By this simple act I set the stage, knowingly or not, for fresh inspiration on a grand scale.

Thanks, Dr. Sagan.

My first selection was *Cosmos*, the classic work by Carl Sagan on which the famous TV series is based. In it, he describes the grandeur of the universe so compellingly, that for weeks I went around telling everyone I knew: hey—do you know there are more stars than all the grains of sand on all the beaches of the planet Earth?

It's ironic. That book, written by a scientist who was himself a passionate denier of all things paranormal, paved the way for my change of heart by initiating a much-needed period of curiosity and wonder in my life. The cosmos it described was so unthinkably huge, and Sagan's prose imbued it with such splendor, that . . . well who's to say what's possible or impossible in such a universe? Or so I suddenly felt.

So when the club offered *The After Death Experience: The Physics of the Non-Physical* by Ian Wilson, I bought it. The "physics" in the title put me at ease. It made me feel that I could join Wilson in his musings without having to question the core assumption that matter is all that matters.

Besides, I thought, what *does* happen to the molecules and atoms of my body when I die? Might they become part of the soil, turn into plants and so forth, and thus have a conscious experience? And might I (whatever "I" really means) somehow participate in that?

As you can see, though intrigued, I was still very much the materialist.

Well, the book turned out to be different than I expected—something altogether better. Writing with a no-nonsense, skeptical tone, Wilson spends half the book describing some of the familiar evidence for survival, only to then debunk it. I appreciated that. (Though as I now see it, some of his arguments are ill-informed.)

Dying and . . . *returning*?

But he also introduced a phenomenon he couldn't explain away—the near-death experience. He said that a not insignificant percentage of the population claims to have had a medical crisis during which they died, and then come back to life. For despite the label in common use, these voyagers insist that what they tasted was not *near*-death, but death itself.

Intrigued, I read further on the subject, and was struck by claims such as "I felt love a thousand times more powerful than I had ever known." When you consider my devotion to a therapy rooted in exploring the deepest of feelings, it's easy to understand why such a statement would capture my attention.

But above all, I was struck by the paradox at the heart of the NDE. Often, these events involve the stopping, or near-stopping, of all bodily functions. (Vital signs recorded in hospital settings confirm this.) Yet during that period, many people later report having had the most life-changing, beautiful—and somehow, the most *real*—experience, they've ever known. How is this possible and what does it mean?

I had no idea, and finding an answer became my project and my passion. Over the next five years I would devour the NDE literature, including the strongest skeptical arguments I could find, and join a group (IANDS) where I met regularly with near-death experiencers. I wanted to hear their stories first-hand and see what sort of people they were.

And I would write notes to myself—hundreds of pages and index cards worth—presenting all sides of the argument, exploring all the various reasons NDE's might, or might not be, actual proof of life after death.

I studied NDE's, in other words, with the same intensity and skepticism I later applied to precognitive dreams. And after a year or two, my initial impression, as you've guessed, was one my former self would have ridiculed: they do indeed seem to be what experiencers know them to be—a taste of life beyond the body.

One caveat: like precognition, the case for the NDE is rich and complex. You need to see the *whole* picture, the many lines of evidence all pointing towards the essential truth of the phenomenon, and that takes more than just reading an article or two. I hope you'll look at some of my suggested sources later in the book and embark on your own journey of discovery.

What NDE's mean to me.

As I became more and more convinced that NDE's were genuine, my outlook began to change. In thinking about my life, for the first time, as playing out on a broader, eternal scale, I realized how much pressure I had been placing on myself. While trying so hard to "make it all happen" here and now in this body, I was feeling enormous guilt for largely failing to do so.

So many missed opportunities, so many weaknesses and character flaws—in short, so many reasons to feel bad about myself.

But now, in coming to see Bruce Siegel as only one part of who I really am—and perhaps a small part at that—I could relax. I could breathe. I could make the best of what I now think of as (in Ron Scolastico's phrase) my earth adventure, while understanding that there are reasons I've chosen to limit my experience here in specific ways.

Yes, my pain was real, but now I could keep it in perspective. And that was made easier, in part, by a new understanding of what it means to be of service, a phrase I once considered an empty platitude, and the joy I was now experiencing as a result of quitting an ill-fitting sales career and instead, sharing my unique gifts (we all have them) as musician and teacher.

For one of the prime messages of the NDE is that giving and receiving really *are* one and the same—a fact made crystal clear to experiencers in what has come to be known as the Life Review.

An inner tug-of-war.

But change is rarely instantaneous and complete, and my own evolution is a case in point. As I said earlier in the book, for a long time, I was suspicious of my new-found optimism and feared that my growing acceptance of the spiritual meant I was going insane—and I mean that literally.

It's not hard to understand why: though the therapeutic community with which I was involved was hardly a cult, I was experiencing some of the same feelings cult members go through as they begin to question parts of their indoctrination.

In particular, I had been taught that sanity requires moving beyond supposed psychological crutches like God and the afterlife. And in questioning that edict,

I feared I was violating a fundamental principle of the therapy, and thus losing my one hope of salvation. (Not salvation in the religious sense, you understand, but salvation nonetheless.)

I was doubly confused because for so many years, the therapy had been—and was continuing to be—a source of strength.

Since then I've come to understand that the two approaches—spirituality and psychology—don't negate each other in the least. Each turns out to be the necessary complement to the other.

But if that seems obvious now, I assure you, back then, I still needed to be convinced.

Straddling the fence on psi.

Spirituality posed another credibility problem as well. It's impossible to read the NDE literature without being inundated by claims of paranormal functioning both during the event and following it (in the form of newfound abilities). To be clear, a supernatural premise is at the very *heart* of the NDE: the notion that consciousness survives the death of the body.

However for years, I simply couldn't make up my mind about psi. And this was despite the fact that I was making friends and acquaintances who were having psychic experiences of all sorts.

But that was exactly the problem—the only evidence I could point to was rooted in *other* people's experiences, not my own.

I needed something to happen to *me*, something beyond the ken of science, an event with enough magic attached to it that I could no longer doubt that psychic phenomena were real. Without that proof, I worried that the positive changes I was making in my life might turn out to be resting on a foundation of sand.

So this is where my adventure with precognition has its beginnings. My mind and heart were now open to seeing what had long eluded me, and what I was now, in fact, eager to experience for myself; I remember my astonishment at stumbling on the first dream I had that I suspected might be psychic. (While that "eager" may seem to jeopardize my objectivity, to toss out hypotheses because they align with our deepest yearnings is to declare our situation hopeless from the start.)

That, in turn, initiated a period of collecting evidence, firming up my experiment, and weighing the pros and cons—all the while remaining acutely aware that my status as a "believer" was very much in question. After a year or two, I even began to suspect I might never get past the point of telling friends, "Well, I just can't decide. As of this moment, I'd have to say the odds are 50-50 that psi is real."

If that sounds like an uncomfortable place to be, it was a chapter in my life when my days were filled with discovery, mystery, excitement, and hope.

And then, one morning, a startling vision appeared to me just before awakening. This dream, the one that finally tipped the scales, is the first one in this book—*Man Beneath the Spinning Blades*. It was my most compelling case up to that point, and with it, the force of the accumulated evidence simply became too great to be denied. (The one-in-four pattern was already beginning to emerge.)

From then on, if I had to place a wager on whether or not precognition is real, there could no longer be any doubt as to where I would put my money. And with that, my last objection to near-death experiencers and their astonishing claims crumbled. For as a proven psychic, wasn't I now, in a sense, a member of the club? Weren't we witnesses for each other, having experienced what science says is impossible? And by so doing, haven't we proven we're not tied to the physical?

That's how I felt, and never again would trust be such a stumbling block.

And today . . .

Because of the continuing tug of my former beliefs, it took a long time for me to feel on truly solid ground with respect to my dreams and their spiritual implications. The process of easing my fear of going crazy, or at the very least of being sadly misguided, has depended, in part, on answering two questions:

Does my new world view seem to be associated with good things coming my way—health, peace, joy, creativity, friendship?

And the flip side: have I proven to myself that precognition is real and not just something I'd *like* to be real?

Having walked this path for twenty-five years now, I can say with confidence that the answer to both questions is: you bet.

24. The Real Subject Here is Consciousness

Feel free to regard what follows as speculation, though for many of us (including near-death experiencers, about whom I'll have more to say in the next chapter) it's more than that.

A book about precognition is a book about time. And it might seem that the focus of our investigation would thus be something external to us, an aspect of reality existing independently of the mind that stops to ponder it.

But such an assumption would miss the mark. For as we've seen, exploring time means looking into *ourselves*. Experiments like mine show that it is in probing our own consciousness that we unlock time's secrets.

And why is this so? Maybe it's because, as some of us are learning, time and consciousness are inseparable. Time, in this view, is actually a dimension of reality created by consciousness *within itself*, so that we might explore certain kinds of experiences.

And the same is true for what we call "space."

Time and space, in other words, are props devised by Mind for much the same reason that storytellers and game designers devise the rules and frameworks that characterize their creations: to spawn worlds within which epic adventures can unfold.

And if this seems like just a fanciful theory, you'd have a hard time convincing Jeannie Dicus of that. In describing what she learned when her heart went into fibrillation and she found herself floating outside her body, she says:

> I was told that before we're born, we have to take an oath that we will pretend time and space are real so we can come here and advance our spirit. (Dicus)

But while this purposeful amnesia with respect to our spiritual origins is productive, it also has a downside. Through it, frustration, and even hopelessness, may arise, as we struggle to make sense of a world in which so many of our basic needs and desires are thwarted.

If what I'm saying is true, it points up the importance of our next chapter. In it, we meet some of the pioneers in the field of what might be called consciousness studies. Their goal: to help us remember what we've forgotten. For in recalling these deeper truths, in discovering that we are more than we think we are, we find reason to trust that the difficulties we face in this life aren't the whole story.

And isn't it good, sometimes, to be reminded of that?

25. Pathfinders, Resources, Further Thoughts

Introducing you to my fellow psi enthusiasts is a pleasure I wouldn't want to miss—a chance not only to discuss relevant research, but to revisit books and authors that have brought more stimulation and inspiration into my life than I can say.

Most of these writers have something in common: each was as astonished as I was to have his or her worldview shattered. And the fact that they're personal favorites is no coincidence—as a former skeptic, it's easier for me to trust those who, like me, began with a dismissive attitude and then gradually traversed the stages of acceptance.

My reading has been sporadic. Just think of what follows as a small sampling of thinkers and researchers who've crossed my path, and to whom I'm grateful.

I'll also offer a caveat as to where *not* to go for unbiased information on psi. Hint: it starts with a W and is a massive and usually helpful online encyclopedia.

My recommendations fall into several groups, the first of which is meant to provide:

A More Balanced View of Precognition

As proof of psi, my dreams are often relatively unimpressive when considered individually. (Though their combined message is clear.) And while the subtlety of my garden-variety examples helps us understand how precognition slips by undetected, it may be misleading to readers who are new to the subject.

Which is why I encourage you to sample the phenomenon in its more robust forms. To that end, the following sources are rich with examples that, like Derek's dream, require no analysis or deciphering of metaphors. They speak for themselves.

- **Dunne, J.W.** *An Experiment in Time*

Dunne's groundbreaking study laid the foundation for my own efforts. You may wish to skip the first several chapters (his story doesn't really get underway until chapter VI) as well as the last, theoretical, section (chapter XV on). What's sandwiched between, though, is a captivating tale of discovery as well as a useful guide for fellow dream explorers.

As of this writing, it's only $.99 at Amazon.

- **Ryback, David.** *Dreams That Come True*

Ryback's work includes a wealth of precognitive dreams presented simply, persuasively, and often with considerable human interest. Highly recommended, and, though out of print, it can be bought second-hand from Amazon.

- **Dossey, Larry.** *The Power of Premonitions*

A comprehensive overview of the subject, including its history and primary investigators. Lots of great examples throughout this fascinating book. Note: for some reason, it's also sold under the name *The Science of Premonitions.*

- **Paquette, Andrew.** *Dreamer*

I got to know Andrew a bit during my years of participating in the Skeptiko. com forum. Like me, he's a former skeptic who eventually became a dedicated explorer and documenter of his own dreams. For sheer quantity, his dream archive puts mine to shame, and many of his examples are definitely *not* garden-variety. In particular, the dream that opens Andrew's book is stunning in its power and detail, and seems clearly (as with Derek's experience) to have enabled him to avoid a sad fate—in this case, being murdered!

- **Graff, Dale.** *Tracks in the Psychic Wilderness*

From 1978 to 1995, the US government ran a top-secret agency devoted to exploiting psi for military purposes. Graff, a former director of the unit, writes largely of his personal explorations over the years. While the book focuses on remote viewing, a number of his experiences involve precognition, and some of those are doozies (as are the non-precognitive ones).

Among others, he devised a protocol (mentioned in the chapter where I provide instructions) using pre-selected targets. As a result, some of his cases resemble some of mine—dreams that come true instantly on awakening.

• Sinclair, Upton. *Mental Radio*

Upton Sinclair was a renowned muckraking author in the first half of the 20th century. This is Sinclair's only foray into parapsychology, and in its German edition, boasts a foreword by no less a figure than Albert Einstein.

Partly because of the author's unquestioned integrity (his success as a writer is based largely on his passion for socially-oriented issues), *Mental Radio* is one of the most persuasive works on psi ever written, and is a delight to read. Numerous experiments carried out by Sinclair and his wife are meticulously presented, with page after page of drawings by the author, shown side-by-side with his wife's psychically intuited matching illustrations.

Like *Tracks in the Psychic Wilderness*, *Mental Radio* is only tangentially devoted to precognition—it occasionally showed up, to the couple's surprise, in the course of their experiment in mental telepathy. You can buy the book for just a couple of dollars at Amazon in the Kindle version—make sure to get an edition that has all the illustrations!

• Sheldrake, Rupert. *Dogs That Know When Their Owners Are Coming Home*

Sheldrake, a biologist trained at both Cambridge and Harvard, points out the shortcomings of mainstream science so persuasively, that one of his books prompted the late Sir John Maddox to call it "the best candidate for burning there has been for many years." (Talk about having one's worldview threatened.)

Dogs That Know details experiments and observations that demonstrate the psychic abilities (including precognition) of a variety of animals. It lays the foundation for his more theoretical works, such as *The Presence of the Past*, a personal favorite.

Support From the Near-Death Experience

My experiment, in and of itself, has shown me that psi is real. No further proof is needed, and if you try the experiment yourself, you may well feel the same.

As to the *ramifications* of precognition—well, that's a separate question. And after reading my conclusions in the chapter called "Why Psi Matters," even those who agree with me up to that point, may feel that I go too far. But as I've said, my confidence in the existence of a spiritual reality stems partly from facts largely unmentioned in this book.

I've talked about one of those influences—the near-death experience. If my insights seem to hang on too slender a thread, I encourage you to look further into this extraordinary phenomenon. NDE's show, among other things, that:

Time as we know it is a *local* phenomenon. NDErs virtually all say that as their physical selves ceased to function, time as they knew it ended. Suddenly, everything seemed to be happening at once, and they tell us that in order to verbalize the event, they're forced to divide a seamless whole into parts.

Though I'm tempted to explain why attributing such statements to poetic license would be a mistake, it would take a whole chapter, or better yet, a book, to do so properly. As with the case for precognition, the NDE is a puzzle with many pieces. Suffice it say that precognitive dreams aren't the only reason to think that we can, under certain circumstances, step outside the time/space continuum.

Consciousness extends beyond the body. If, while lying in bed, I can visit, or demonstrate that I already exist in, the future, that means I am more than a physical being. Few facts have such power to transform our lives, and if you're looking for further verification, you need look no further than the NDE.

NDErs say that the term used to categorize their experience doesn't go far enough. Rather than *nearly* dead, they describe themselves as having been *temporarily* dead. It's an important distinction, and those who flat-line within hospital settings often have the medical records to back up their claim.

If they're right, then anything we experience during an NDE happens beyond the physical. And as the literature shows, vital signs are far from the whole story in terms of proving that the out-of-body experience (OBE) is just what its name suggests.

But I invite you to check out the following sources for other reasons as well. Having written a book that focuses largely on evidence, I encourage you now to explore its life-changing implications, and these authors help us do just that. (With a spiritual, as opposed to religious, slant.)

So read, enjoy, be inspired.

• **Moody, Raymond.** *Life After Life*

Near-death experiences have been reported throughout history. But Moody, by giving the phenomenon the perfect name and codifying its main characteristics, single-handedly set in motion an entire field of studies in the last decades of the 20th century.

Free of hype and refreshingly modest, *Life After Life* is a straightforward telling of the author's investigations. In that respect it's like *An Experiment in Time—*both writers stumbled on a phenomenon they couldn't explain, and have gifted us by sharing their adventure in unraveling it.

Check out also *Glimpses of Eternity*, Moody's book on a special category of NDE: ones that were simultaneously experienced or shared by loved ones who were *not* in physical distress. In many cases, these witnesses acquired veridical (provable) knowledge about the dying person that they were later able to verify.

• **Ring, Kenneth.** *Lessons From The Light.*

After Moody got the NDE ball rolling, Ring was one of the first to expand on his findings. With his uniquely balanced approach, he sheds light on matters psychological, parapsychological, and spiritual. I especially like how, by taking the time to help us get to know each individual experiencer, Ring gets us emotionally involved in their post-NDE transformations.

• **Sabom, Michael.** *Recollections of Death*

Sabom is a cardiologist who was initially skeptical of Moody's claims in *Life After Life*. He wondered why, if the phenomenon were so widespread, none of his patients, some of them temporary flat-liners themselves, had reported it.

So he began asking them, and found that though many were indeed having such encounters, they were reluctant to share their experience with someone from the medical profession, a group not particularly known (especially back in the 1970's and 80's) for its open-mindedness towards such things.

The studies Sabom subsequently carried out are compelling. Having access to hospital records, he knew exactly what had happened during patients' resuscitations, and was astonished to hear them describe in detail unusual procedures, instruments, and other specifics impossible for them to have seen under ordinary circumstances.

- **Long, Jeffrey.** *Evidence of the Afterlife: The Science of Near-Death Experiences.*

    With his wife Jody, Dr. Jeffrey Long established in the 1990's a website that now houses thousands of NDE accounts (linked to below). Based on what he's learned from this mountain of data, his book explores nine lines of evidence that all point to the conclusion that the NDE is just what it seems: a glimpse of life beyond the body.

- **Moorjani, Anita.** *Dying to Be Me*

    In her moving memoir, Moorjani describes how, apparently thanks to an NDE, her life was spared from the ravages of a cancer she was not expected to survive. Medically, psychologically, and spiritually, this is one remarkable account.

    To name just a few of those who've written compellingly about their NDEs: Eben Alexander, Nancy Danison, Natalie Sudman, Betty Eadie, Marion Rome, and the man whose experience was the impetus for Moody's research, George Ritchie.

Dealing With Skepticism and Wikipedia

Since so many of us rely on Wikipedia, a special caveat seems in order. The encyclopedia's *site-wide* policy is that parapsychology is a pseudoscience—a science without a subject. They say there simply *is no evidence for psi,* nothing worth talking about.

So be forewarned. While you might think such a prestigious resource as Wikipedia would encourage contributors to express diverse views, when it comes to the paranormal only one conclusion is tolerated. Facts supporting psi are either removed, presented in their weakest form, or kept to a minimum and overwhelmed by a larger number of opposing points.

- **McLuhan, Robert.** *Randi's Prize*

    In this beautifully written book, McLuhan debunks the debunkers. As he details cases representing a variety of apparently anomalous phenomena, he shows how, time and again, skeptical objections that seem at first to devastate the pro-psi position, fall woefully short.

- **Carter, Chris.** *Science and Psychic Phenomena: The Fall of the House of Skeptics*

Like McLuhan, Carter has mastered the skeptical position and is well-qualified to refute it. Oxford-trained, and speaking calmly, intelligently, and with little of the smugness or sarcasm often found in books by Randi, Dawkins, et al, his writings are a counterbalance to the one-sided presentations on Wikipedia.

- **Weiler, Craig.** *PSI Wars: TED, Wikipedia and the Battle for the Internet*

Though I haven't read Craig's book yet, I participated in online discussions in which he talked about his then work-in-progress. What follows is from an Amazon review of *Psi Wars* by Dean Radin, one of our most distinguished parapsychologists, and as you'll see, a trenchant observer in his own right:

> [This book] describes a world where the most widely accessed factual encyclopedia is actually a work of fantasy written by anonymous amateurs; where organizations that purport to support scientific inquiry in fact do the complete opposite; where a celebrated science prize is actually an impossible-to-win publicity stunt; and where an entertainment outlet with a mission for sharing ideas instead acts to censor them.

Online Resources

- **Michael Prescott's Blog**

http://michaelprescott.typepad.com/michael_prescotts_blog/

Like me, Michael came late to a spiritual worldview, and his blog is, to some extent, a record of his own philosophical journey. Michael's work serves as a model for how to discuss psi and metaphysics with clarity, grace, and respect for all points of view; dialoguing with Michael and his commenters for the past fifteen years has helped to shape the writer I am.

(A visit to his blog triggered—retroactively, of course—one of the dreams in this book—*The Round Object That Merged With a Flat Surface.*)

- **Alex Tsakiris's Skeptiko**

http://www.skeptiko-forum.com/

I used to participate regularly on Alex's site too. In addition to his vast archive of interviews with the top names in parapsychology—proponents *and* skeptics—Alex provides a nicely organized community forum. Membership is free, and visitors can take part in a wide variety of ongoing discussions. (The first glimmerings of this book appeared in a thread I started on Skeptiko many years ago.)

Alex has written *Why Science is Wrong . . . About Almost Everything*. A bit over the top? (The title, I mean.) Well, that's Alex—never one to shy from controversy.

• Robert McLuhan's Paranormalia

Besides having written the already-mentioned *Randi's Prize*, Robert maintains his own blog. One chapter of *Dreaming the Future* first appeared, in a different form, as a guest post on his site. Thanks for getting me started, Robert!

• Psi Encyclopedia

http://psi-encyclopedia.spr.ac.uk/

Devoted to the entire spectrum of psychic abilities, Psi Encyclopedia is yet another reason for readers to feel grateful to Robert McLuhan, whose work as editor has shepherded it into existence. Among its archives:

http://psi-encyclopedia.spr.ac.uk/articles/precognition-0

This 18,000-word article in particular is likely to be of interest to readers of this book. Contributed by Robert Rosenberg, it looks at the history of the research into precognition, and includes examples of the phenomenon from a variety of sources.

• NDERF.org

This is Dr. Jeffrey Long's site, referred to earlier. In the section entitled "NDE Stories," you might want to start with the "Exceptional" category. As many of these as I've read, I never tire of checking out the latest accounts. More often than not, each experiencer will have his or her own unique take, with observations that fascinate, enlighten, comfort, or move.

• SkepticalAboutSkeptics.org

Lots of good info here, much of it devoted to Wikipedia.

A final recommendation.

- **Grof, Stanislav.** *The Cosmic Game.*

For a fuller account of the sort of universe I've been hinting at, read this masterful book. Quite simply, no one is better than Grof at explaining *how it all works*. In particular, his insights into the importance—the necessity, really—of evil and suffering, are indispensable.

On a personal note, it was Grof, who, by reconciling psychotherapy and spirituality, helped me to see my way forward.

26. My Invitation To You

In these pages I've picked up the thread of precognition from where Dunne and others have left it, and now it's up to you, my readers, to write the next chapter.

Because I'm in Dunne's shoes. Having satisfied himself that precognition was real, he asked his friends to record their own dreams (as he tells us in *An Experiment With Time*). Would they get the same results? To a remarkable extent, they did.

So I extend a similar invitation. Do we all dream of the future or only some of us? You can help us get to the truth of the matter.

As to why, a hundred years after Dunne, so little progress has been made in answering this question, or even in convincing science that *anyone*, much less everyone, is psychic, I have a theory. Perhaps, as we come into the physical plane (as we enter the womb, in other words), we agree to hide from ourselves key aspects of our true nature.

Why, you ask? For the challenge, and ultimately the thrill, of re-discovering them! Maybe this cloaking and gradual uncloaking of our original nature, is at the very heart of the earth adventure.

If so, it stands to reason that there may always be those who believe in such things as psi, and those who don't.

In any case, if you try the experiment, whatever your results, I look forward to hearing from you, and promise to report back on the results of this survey. Happy psi-hunting!

***

Share your experience on my blog at BruceSiegel.net, or contact me personally at Bruce@BruceSiegel.net.

APPENDICES

Appendix A: *The Man Beneath the Spinning Blades*

A question that may be on the minds of some readers is whether I'm presenting both the dream and the video in good faith, or if I'm cherry-picking isolated parts.

So about the video . . .

As is usually the case, the waking event is concise—a 23-second stretch of tape near the start of the news segment that accounts for all the correlations we've discussed. And cherry-picking can't be much of a factor because 18 of the 23 seconds portray what you see in photos 1-4 (allowing for the copter's continued movement between those four frames).

As to the dream . . .

What follows is the entire transcript. (I've numbered the paragraphs for easy reference.) It's rambling and redundant, but it shows that the quotes I selected paint an accurate picture of the dream.

Complete unedited transcript, as recorded on 8/1/93.

[1] "It's 7:10 A.M. I just woke up from a dream with an unusual image in it. It's about this flying machine that is like . . . almost like a flying fan (as in a fan that spins and keeps your room cool). It's this small flying machine that is designed for amateurs to fly, and it consists of kind of like helicopter-type blades . . . kind of similar to that."

[2] "There's not really too much to this contraption -- the blades

spinning overhead and you sitting below them. And I just have a strong image of seeing this guy fly down a street. I was amazed at how close he was flying to the . . . and how close the rotors were going to . . . he was just flying about ten feet off the road perhaps . . .but the rotors of the blades were coming really close to like telephone poles on the side. And I was surprised at how close they were coming. I was thinking how can he maneuver this down the center of the street without touching occasionally."

[3] "I was thinking you have to get used to the *size* of the spinning blades. Kind of like when you learn to drive you have to get used to the size of the car -- how big it is from side to side."

[4] "That's the dream about this flying helicopter-almost for . . . amateurs."

[5] "So this dream is about this flying fan-almost for amateur pilots. And I see an image of this guy going down the road close to both sides. Even though this thing is really for one person, I have an image that he's got a woman with him that he's taking for this . . . joy-ride."

[6] "In the flight just before they had gone higher, but in this one they're going pretty low. Not *they*—in the flight before it was just one person— he was going high . . . or someone else going high. But in this flight there's a woman in it."

Discrepancies (superficial and real).

My transcript talks about "like telephone poles" rather than wires. But as I've said, if a helicopter were flying as described, it would be hemmed in by power lines, precisely as pictured in photo #3.

A more legitimate discrepancy is that there's an apparent miss (or Mrs.) near the end of paragraph 5. (I refer to her again at the end of paragraph 6.) Clearly, no woman is to be seen in the photos.

However, this news story was warmly introduced by a female anchor, saying, in effect: whatever they pay this guy, it's not enough. So you might say that at least in spirit, a woman *was* along for the ride.

Does that explain the woman mentioned in my dream? I can't really say.

In any case, note that no woman is mentioned until very late in the transcript. That's significant because when recording my dreams, I always begin with what seems most important. Secondary matters are mentioned later, after all the key points have been safely documented before vanishing from memory. So the fact that the main body of the transcript—like the video—focuses on a lone male, tells us something.

Other points to consider:

• As I've said, I didn't see a cabin or enclosure, so I didn't understand that what I was being shown was a real helicopter.

• It's clear from the transcript that I thought the man who was visible *outside* the craft was piloting it. Obviously, in the waking event, he wasn't.

Now these last items are clear discrepancies, but keep in mind that when we dream about actual events from the *past*, we also typically omit key aspects or incorporate fantasy elements.

Be that as it may, it should be clear by now that the hits are no mirage: most of what's contained in this strange dream is true for the real-life event too.

Four hits without proper documentation—take 'em or leave 'em.

With respect to all my cases, all the correlations on which my statistics rest are drawn from dream data that was recorded before the waking events.

Sometimes, though, while experiencing a predicted event, I'll remember corresponding aspects of the dream that, for one reason or another, I failed to document. This happens fairly often because trying to record every last detail would take too long.

But I repeat: no matter how convincing an unrecorded hit may be, it is *never* taken into consideration when scoring a dream.

Here are four additional correlations for this case—items I clearly remembered but which are not referred to in the transcript. I jotted them down while watching the video the day of the dream—while its details were still fresh in my mind—and archived them separately from the rest.

In the dream:

1. Initially, the man and his flying machine were resting on the ground. (As we see in photo #1.)

2. As he rose into the air, the direction of movement was left to right. (If I were to include the frame(s) immediately following photo #2, this aspect would be clearly visible.)

3. The blades were positioned above, and somewhat *behind* the man. (Which of course is also the case in the photos.) It was as though they were somehow *strapped* to his upper back, which is not at all logical, but hey—this is a dream, right?

4. At some point, the plane of the spinning blades changed, as their front or back tips (at this point I can't remember which) dipped. (See photo #2.)

Compared to other hits, these four points involve variables that are more commonplace (which is why it seemed less important to document them in the first place). Still, each adds another layer of improbability. Though the case is strong even without these unrecorded matches, they were crystal-clear in my mind as I watched the video, and added considerably to my astonishment.

(This is the Appendix to chapter 5. Move on now to Chapter 6.)

Appendix B: *Fallen Limb, Long Odds*

Complete unedited transcript, as recorded on 7/1/2011.

"Some large plant, it's not quite a tree, but the stem is hard and woody, and a significant portion of it has fallen down, And I'm thinking that it has to be . . . .there's nothing left of it standing . . . . there's virtually nothing left of it that's good and standing. It'll have to be carted off. I'm thinking--Oh jeez, I'll have to cut it up into sections and put it at the curb, because it's big and needs to be disposed of. Do I want to hire someone or do it myself?

As I'm looking at it I see someone at Sam's place who is perhaps cutting up . . . a person who's like a gardener . . . and I think they're disposing of the same plant somehow, or a similar one, and I'm thinking about that gardener . . . I see them somehow at the fence of Sam's yard that touches on the alley, right near their shed. I'm thinking, should I pay this person to do the work of cutting this plant up and disposing of it?"

What I missed.

I've explained that in my dream, the gardener at Sam's place was a figment of my imagination, probably a symbol of the help I would have liked to receive. In addition, in the dream, I didn't understand that what I was seeing was actually a tree limb. I simply never grasped that part of the equation, though what I saw certainly *resembles* a limb: "some large plant, it's not quite a tree, but the stem is hard and woody."

Notice the similarity, in this respect, to the spinning blades dream, in which I also missed a key aspect—the presence of a full-fledged helicopter. I think it's fair to say that both dreams captured the essence of the waking event, while leaving me in the dark about the true context.

As you'll see, this sort of selective focus is one of the characteristics of the phenomenon that allows it to go largely unnoticed.

(This is the Appendix to Chapter 7. Move on now to Chapter 8.)

Appendix C: *The Round Object That Merged With A Flat Surface*

Though I originally documented this vision over a year ago, I continue to have new insights. While writing it up for this book, I was amazed to see a major correlation that had eluded my previous brainstorming. (The throwing technique, as already discussed.)

As a result, I think I can now make sense of all the discrepancies except one: the substitution of a ceiling for a wall. But if you think about the vast universe of potential targets, the two begin to seem virtually identical.

You don't need to be impressed by what follows to be convinced that precognition is at work here. Based solely on the facts as already presented, the case is strong.

First, a brief sidebar: Up to my early twenties I was an avid tennis player, and back then, the balls were all white. And because I would use the same ones for years (often for baseball-related games), the felt was always beaten down flat. So when I think "tennis ball," I automatically picture a smooth, off-white sphere. You'll see the importance of this in a moment.

The image that got sent into the past.

Put yourself in my shoes as I tried to visualize the professor's scenario. Imagine that you're perhaps eight feet from a wall, watching a tennis ball you've just tossed, go through the wall in slow motion, without damaging it.

Remember: you're primarily focused on the ball *entering* the wall, because you can't see the ball as it exits the other side, and there's little reason to picture the ball in your hand, or as it arcs towards the wall. Sights like those are routine—

you want to see the impossible.

When most of the ball is engulfed, freeze-frame the action. What you see, will look like image #3 below:

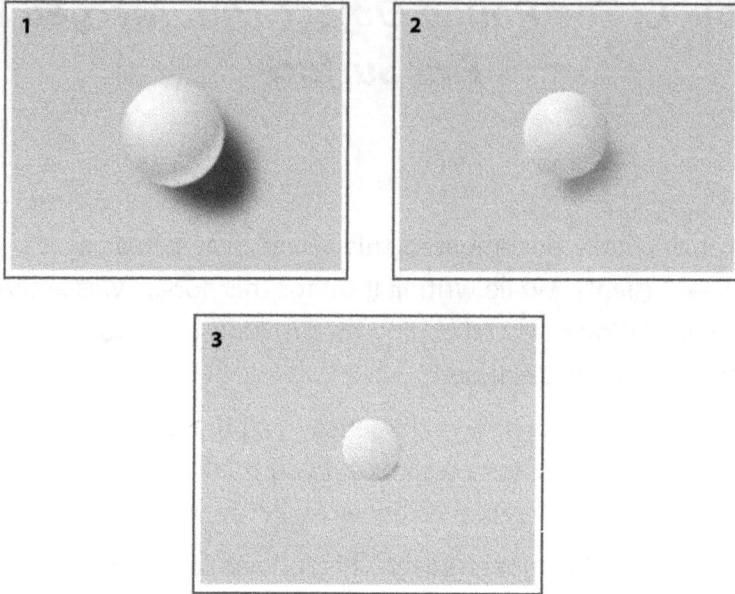

As the ball nearly disappears and its three-dimensional curvature becomes hard to make out, doesn't the protruding part begin to look disk-like? And when just a tiny sliver is visible, mightn't it even look thin and papery? Remember—to me, a tennis ball is a relatively smooth, off-white, thing.

So (except for the ceiling/wall tradeoff) *this* is the image I previewed while meditating two hours earlier. And since my vision showed what seemed to be a disk-like object adhering to the ceiling, I assumed that's what I had just thrown. After all, no one expects to see a ball inside a ceiling. So it's understandable I would have jumped to the more logical conclusion—something was stuck *on* it.

(In the original vision, the ceiling was high, which would have made it harder to make out detail, and easier to misinterpret what I was seeing.)

If I'm right—if I, like the professor, was actually throwing a ball—then the case obviously becomes even more impressive.

And remember, other evidence backs up this theory. The underhand throwing technique my vision painstakingly documents makes no sense at all if I'm tossing a thin, papery, disk. But for an object the approximate size and shape of a ball, it's perfect.

Complete unedited transcript, as recorded on 2/12/2014

"I had an image. I think it was me . . . I was tossing disks, trying to get them to stick on the ceiling. These were like . . . disk is not the right word . . . more like pieces of paper . . . circular pieces of paper or . . . thin material like that . . . maybe a couple of inches in diameter. . . and I was tossing them, trying to get them to stick on the ceiling.

I put that in the plural. It might have been just one I was trying to get up, I don't know. I don't know if it was one or if it was more. Certainly just one at a time.

The motion that I was using . . . it was like the disk was in the . . . like resting on my fingers, as my hand was hanging at my side. Resting on my fingers like on the inner surface of my hand, and it was kind of like an underhand heave up to the ceiling trying to get this disk or disks to, one at a time, to stick flat on the ceiling."

Blog comment excerpt (the matching event).

"What we are going to study in this class is basically equivalent to **me throwing a tennis ball against this concrete wall and every now and then it goes through**."

(This is the Appendix to Chapter 9. Move on now to Chapter 10.)

Appendix D: *The Student Loan*

What I've presented in the main chapter is all that's necessary to categorize this case as strong. In what follows, I'll present additional correlations which imply a slight shift in the metaphor. (A situation I discuss a bit further on.) In keeping with other appendices, feel free to make of these additional hits what you will.

At the heart of both dream and event is a dispute over ownership. I begin my dream narrative (presented in its entirety at the end of this appendix) by saying that despite my teacher's claim, I think the music score is mine. Likewise, when Rubio asks "Who is Hilary Clinton to lecture me about repaying students loans?" what he means is: don't be misled by what she's telling you—this is *my* turf.

In other words, the question in the dream is: who owns the score? And in the event: who owns the campaign issue?

The metaphor is apt. Music scores and campaign issues are both bread and butter essentials within their respective professions. A musician needs sheet music to perform, just as a politician can't win votes without a platform or agenda.

So let's pick up the correlations from where we left off. Remember, the waking event is **"Who is Hillary Clinton to lecture me about repaying students loans?"**

9. **The crux of the scene is the matter of who is the rightful owner** . . . (The first sentence of the transcript is: "I'm waking up from a dream that has to do with who owns a copy of some piano music.")

10. . . . . **of something central to the performance of their shared profession. (**The score; the campaign issue.**)**

11. **The younger person feels the item is his because of his long and unique history with it.** (Rubio's well-publicized personal experience with loans is symbolized by my lengthy hands-on relationship with the book,

as evidenced by it now containing all my precious fingering. You pianists will relate.)

    12. **He says that the older person is not as deeply involved with the item as he is.** (From the dream: "he's done without it for this long, so why does he need it now?")

    13. **The younger person asks: what is this person's justification for claiming ownership?** (In the dream: "I think I actually asked him, what's the advantage [to you] of having this copy?")

More about "the book" and what it represents.

These additional hits imply that the music score has a dual meaning. While for the correlations listed in the main chapter it represents money borrowed, for these, it stands for the campaign issue. (These two meanings are not so far apart: for the skilled politician, the perfect campaign issue is like money in the bank.)

While this adds a complication I don't remember seeing in other cases, in a fascinating twist, the dream itself seems to be alerting us to the fact that the book represents more than one thing:

    "I'm aware of . . . oh, there are two . . . I'm actually holding two music books in my hand. It's funny because at first I thought there was just a single book, then I realized that it's actually two."

This delayed understanding neatly mirrors my two-stage process as I analyzed the case.

And there's more:

    "They [the music books] definitely have a soft cover. . . I'm thinking that one of them is red. That color is coming to my mind."

Now I don't speak Spanish, and while I've learned since having the dream that "rubio" means yellow, previously it always brought to my mind one color only, and strongly at that: ruby red.

And if you think this is getting far-fetched, then note this:

"I'm realizing that it's a foreign edition . . . it's something that I would have to order from overseas."

Get it? The book, like Marco Rubio (to my mind), is red and foreign. (Rubio's parents both immigrated from Cuba, making him the most "foreign" of the presidential candidates.)

If these last correlations are valid, then the book has taken on a *third* function—it symbolizes the senator himself.

As I've said, a multi-functioning metaphor would be new to me. But then, I'm continually making fresh discoveries about how precognition manifests in my dreams. If you suspect I'm making too much of any of the points I've raised in the appendix, though, keep in mind that the case is strong even without them.

More about the CNN article

The location of Rubio's comment within the piece means that there was about three minutes worth of reading before I got to it. Nothing in the preceding text remotely resembles the dream, and the same can be said of the few emails I quickly glanced at just before reading it.

And that's it. In that brief 12-minute span, there was virtually no other opportunity for a matching event. As I've said, I got up, went to another room, and quickly glanced at a few incoming emails. At that time of day, I don't listen to the radio, watch TV, or have other people with me.

Complete unedited transcript, as recorded on 8/7/2015

As I give you the whole, long, rambling, text to read, I confess that it's sometimes hard for me to grasp that "Who is Hilary Clinton to lecture me about repaying students loans?" turned into *this* dream.

But it did. Given the many correlations, and especially the timing, there's little room for doubt.

Just remember that in the waking event, Rubio speaks of: **student; borrowing;** and a **disagreement about ownership** (of the issue). And *every word* in the transcript of the dream is spoken by a **student**, about something he **borrowed**, and a **conflict about who owns it**.

Can there be a better example of evidence that hides in plain sight?

"I'm waking up from a dream that has to do with who owns a copy of some piano music. I'm talking with someone who seems like . . it's either Mr. Plumley or some similar figure. The situation is he's . . . I have a copy of a score, and I've evidently just finished working on a piece in the book with him. And essentially, he's claiming that I borrowed it from him, and I'm thinking that I didn't. I'm thinking that it's mine.

So I say to him, well, you know, I'm not sure who's right about this but how about if I just get you a new copy of it, because this one has all my fingering in it. I'll just get you a new copy.

And he's reluctant to do that. So I'm really surprised. I think I actually asked him, what's the advantage of having this copy?

I was thinking of a joke, though I didn't make it, but I'm thinking the joke—Ahhh you wanna have a copy I've actually been using so that when I'm famous it'll be worth something.

In the dream I'm aware of . . . Oh, there are two . . .I'm actually holding two music books in my hand. It's funny because at first I thought there was just a single book, then I realized that it's actually two. They definitely have a soft cover. They might be like a Kalmus edition but they're not that green color, they're . . . I'm thinking that one of them is red. That color is coming to my mind.

As I said, I'm surprised that I'm actually holding two books in my hand, and I'm realizing that it's a foreign edition . . . OK so that doesn't make sense, because then it wouldn't be Kalmus. The it's something that I would have to order from overseas, so it would take some time, and I think it also occurred to me that that might be why he wants this copy -- so that he can have it right away. Yes, that occurred to me in the dream.

Now I'm just a bit peeved that he's making a big issue of this because I've obviously had the book for a long time as I was working on it. For this reason, I've had the book for a long time, number 2 I'm not even really sure that it's his, 3, I've had if for so long that it has all my fingering in it for this piece in question, and also maybe for other pieces in it.

Those 3 reasons . . . the question of who actually owns it, the fingering, and the fact that he's done without it for this long, so why does he need it now?

For those three reasons I'm a little disappointed, you know, that he's making a big thing about this.

I certainly don't remember anything like this happening with Mr. Plumley or any other teacher, I just don't remember it, but I'm recording the dream because it's unusual, and there are some really good specifics in it.

It was happening just before waking up . . . and I'm wide awake now. I think I actually fell asleep while meditating. And then slept for a while. I'm ready to go about my day right now, so it's the sort of thing where it could be precognitive because I'm about to go on the internet and proceed with my day."

(This is the Appendix to Chapter 14. Move on now to Chapter 15.)

Appendix E: *The Honey-Trap Mystery*

Given a characteristic of the phenomenon we've seen repeatedly, it makes sense that this precognitive dream targeted my reading of the phrase "honey-trap." Because besides having a new expression to ponder, I was titillated. In the minutes that passed since recording the dream, it's likely that nothing grabbed my attention as undividedly as picturing what sort of "honey" that French actress might have used to tempt poor Francois.

So why, you may ask, didn't the dream reflect the sexual aspect? Because, as we saw in *Student Loan*, precognitive dreams often *play* with real-life events rather than capture them literally—they latch on to words and images and explore meanings for them that are new and unexpected. If you think about it, my dream operated as a double-entendre in reverse (considering the typically naughty nature of this form of wordplay)—it took a sexual innuendo and cleaned it up!

What a dullard *I* turned out to be.

Compare this waking event to a later potential match.

A little more than five months after documenting this dream, I was watching a TV adaptation of *War and Peace*. In one scene, a female character says to her friend, "It takes a lot of honey to trap a big fly." Her point was that a woman needs to go to considerable lengths to attract a particularly eligible bachelor.

Naturally, I thought of the *Honey Trap* case, and wondered if this was a second match for the dream (a situation that does sometimes occur, and which I discuss in a later chapter.) For several reasons, I have little reason to think it is. As you may recall, the 3-part "pun" in this case is on the complete thought: "In the context of a mystery, a honey trap may do harm to the unaware." And while a honey trap is indeed present in *War and Peace*, the tale is not a mystery, nor is catching a husband normally thought of as bringing harm to the ensnared. (Though opinions on that may vary—particularly along gender lines.)

In any case, I've yet to mention perhaps the most important point: the timing. This second honey trap showed up on my radar *five months* after the dream, in contrast to the first, which appeared in mere minutes. Because of the lengthy interim, and keeping in mind that I assign a "2" to what I consider my proven cases, and a "1" to dreams that *may* be precognitive, this second event fails to provide the sort of evidence that would motivate me to consider a dream even a "maybe." It doesn't even come close. (Just to show you how I think about these things.)

I mention all this because thanks to the later event, it becomes clearer than ever what a stunning match that sentence in the newspaper review truly was.

The dream, unedited.

In the following endlessly redundant transcript (me at my most obsessive), I've bolded all the references to "honey" and "mystery," as well as the sections that explain why the situation is hazardous (a trap).

"Sunday August 30th, 7:36 AM.

So I just woke up from a dream with an unusual element. Nothing routine here whatsoever.

I'm part of a family here. And we are learning . . . we're getting the answer to a question . . . a **mystery** that has long kept us **puzzled**.

It turns out that when we originally moved to our house, we treated the earth—I guess it's the ground where our lawn now is—we somehow saturated it with **honey**. We made some kind of mistake at that time and oversaturated the earth with **honey**. And that explains why you had a certain amazingly abundant growth of some plant over the years—I'm thinking some kind of tree or some kind of plant over the years has been amazingly abundant, I mean like in historic proportions. We've had a yield of a certain plant. Because of this **honey** that was initially mistakenly applied.

Now this plant is edible or has an edible aspect to it. Because we eat this plant and the plant itself is **honey**-filled or has a high **honey** content."

Something important about this dream is that what we're learning explains this long-time **mystery** that has always kept us **wondering**. *Ahhh*—so now we understand why we have this overabundant growth of this **honey**-filled plant.

Now, we're learning at this moment the dangers of over-consuming this plant. And some person is educating us specifically as to the problems we're gonna face over the years as we consume this plant, this honey-filled plant in great quantities. And this person is talking to each member of my family .

There are no people in this dream that I'm familiar with. I'm part of a family or family-like group and **our family is being informed person by person . . . One person—I'm thinking it's a woman—I'm thinking that a woman is—I'm not sure about that—I'm thinking that a woman is telling each person in my family how . . . the problem they might have over the years because of eating this honey. And it's different for each of us.**

For some reason, each of us has a different prognosis based on our honey consumption. It's more of a problem for some of us than others. I'm thinking for me, it's not gonna be much of a problem because I don't eat that much **honey**. It's not so much that I don't like it but I just am disciplined in that way so I don't eat too much **honey**.

So I'm recording this dream because I don't remember ever having a dream that contains **honey**. And the **honey**-saturated earth . . . I'm a little confused as to whether the earth was actually saturated with **honey**, or saturated with something that produces the **honey**-filled plant. I have zero doubt that the resulting plant is **honey**-filled, because that's the question: **what problems will we face in eating the honey.**

Of course it logically doesn't make sense that . . . saturating the earth with **honey**. But that's the best I can do, remembering this.

Something else towards the beginning, where we're learning about how we treated the earth, was that the **honey** that we over-applied was like in layers going deep into the earth. There were like layers of it, that were . . . the **honey**, or whatever it was that was applied in layers deep in the earth, at various layers or levels.

So in case I wasn't clear about this, we over-applied . . . In treating the earth initially, we put in too much **honey** or whatever, and that's exactly the substance that this **honey**-producing plant thrives on. It thrives on this stuff that we over-injected into the ground, and that's why we get this plant. That's the **mystery** solved."

(This is the Appendix to *Honey Trap* in Chapter 17. Move on now to the rest of the chapter.)

Appendix F: Bowling and Reincarnation

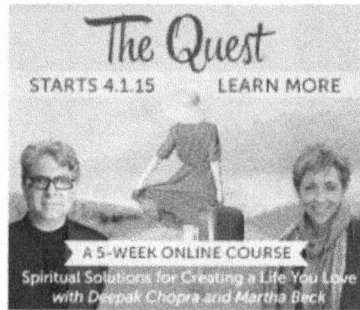

More on the "blade" metaphor.

Though I now consider the blade-related visual pun compelling, it took me a while to take it seriously. That's because the dream is partially incorrect as to the location of the blade, which it says is in:

". . . almost like an opening in a small tunnel roughly the size of the area where the pins are in a bowling alley . . . "

Clearly, the "blade" in the photo is not inside anything, so the dream was just plain wrong about that. But take another look at this:

" . . . you somehow hurl yourself down this lane. . . When you hit this blade headfirst, you die. The blade is . . . like a single blade on a helicopter but it's spinning in a vertical plane rather than a horizontal plane. I'm not even sure that it's spinning but maybe it is."

Notice how much the dream got *right*:

- If the "blade" in the photo were spinning, it would indeed spin in a *vertical* plane (like an airplane propeller).
- As predicted, the blade is in *front* of the "bowler," seemingly at least somewhat farther down the lane, and . . .
- It is perfectly positioned at her head.

Now tell me: have you ever heard of anyone intentionally advancing head-first into a blade of any kind? I hope not—I certainly haven't.

Yet the woman in the photo looks like she's about to do exactly that.

One final thought and we'll wrap this up:

How death entered the picture.

In reading the email, I was anxious to skip the formalities, so I quickly zeroed in on the *middle* of the text, and the first words I saw, weirdly enough, were "a Life You Love ends tonight at midnight Pacific Time." I circled those words in the image above to show that they're located precisely in the center of the paragraph—just where you'd expect my eyes to race to for the meat of the message.

I suspect that my dream picked up on that misreading, and played with it by presenting an intentional, choreographed, death. This would make sense since, as we now know, what matters is not so much the literal content of a waking event, but how my mind *processed* it.

If I'm right, it's pretty cool how my dreaming self took such a lethal theme and built from it a scenario that matches the inspiring mood and content of the rest of the ad.

Complete, unedited, dream text.

If I weren't intent on providing every last shred of documentation, I would edit this. It's embarrassing. It's me at my compulsive-obsessive worst, so afraid of leaving out any potential hit, that I repeat myself endlessly. So don't let its sheer length mislead you—every bit of information contained in what follows could probably be captured in a single well-written page (instead of three).

"Tuesday March 17 9:28 AM. It's been a long time since I've recorded a dream. This one is really interesting. And powerful.

I'm with some friends and we're engaged in an activity that has some resemblance to *bowling* [spoken with an inflection that indicates surprise]. Certainly not that it *is* bowling. Somehow in the physical setup . . . because the person engaged in it . . . the person performing the activity, his body becomes somewhat like the bowling ball in that, here's what happens:

You're facing towards what's almost like a single lane in a bowling alley. Although certainly you're not in a bowling alley. But you're facing towards a run-up towards a . . . almost like an opening in a small tunnel roughly the size of the area where the pins are in a bowling alley.

So it's like you somehow hurl yourself down this lane that is somehow similar to a bowling alley lane towards this opening of a tunnel and you yourself, after going down this lane, enter this opening in which there's something like a single blade . . . maybe it's spinning, but if it's spinning then the blade is positioned vertically almost like a single blade on a helicopter but it's spinning in a vertical plane rather than a horizontal plane. I'm not even sure that it's spinning but maybe it is.

When your body . . . when you hit this blade headfirst, you die. I'm not sure if that's the outcome every time someone engages in this activity or this . . .almost like a sport . . . but if it's not a sure thing that you're gonna die then it's a routine part of this activity. It's like it's the purpose of this activity.

I'll say this again. So it's like you hurl yourself down this lane, which is roughly the length of a bowling alley lane . . . how you go down there . . . "hurl yourself" doesn't make much sense, I understand that, and . . . it's how you choose to move down this lane quickly towards the opening in this sort of like a tunnel in the wall, and get chewed up by this blade which I think may be spinning, as I said on a vertical plane, and it ends your life.

The thing is, people are participating in this activity . . . I'm just with a couple of friends, it seems, and each one is participating in this activity.

In talking about it it's clear that it takes some courage to do this but the others seem to able to do this, to end their life in this way. This is not at all like a tragic scene. This is like something you choose to do. You end your life with the sure knowledge that you come back in another form. In other words, you reincarnate.

But I'm aware, each of us is aware that it takes some courage to do this, and I'm wondering whether I have the courage to do this. I'm scared. And wondering if I have the courage to do this and thinking that maybe I don't.

And I wake up right at the point where I'm thinking, I don't know if I can do this right now. Maybe I need to say goodbye . . . since this is gonna end . . . oh, it's like I'm saying this is the end of Bruce and maybe . . . so as I'm waking up I'm thinking maybe I need to say good-bye to my friends before I do this because this is the end of Bruce. And maybe what's holding me back is that I haven't said goodbye to anybody.

This little quote 'tunnel' or hole in the wall is just big enough for a body to fit into. Almost like a garbage disposal. But it is spinning on a vertical plane rather than a horizontal plane. I don't know what the inside of a garbage disposal looks like but the similarity is that there must be some blade spinning in there and it disposes of whatever goes in as does this hole in the wall towards which your body is speeding.

I'm not clear on the motion that your body is . . . on what it is that propels your body down this quote 'bowling alley lane.' Not a real logic to this but somehow you make the decision and somehow your body goes speeding down this lane towards this opening. And as soon as you enter the opening you immediately hit this device that ends your life. Someone says yes, it's painless. I remember someone describing it, saying don't worry about this. It is painless. It's over quickly.

So my feeling during this dream . . . it's strange, this is not like a nightmare in that there's this horrible . . . that I feel horrible and out of control and like a helpless victim. Not at all.

This is an activity that we're choosing to participate in. It's a *constructive* activity that requires courage but this sort of death is not a tragedy. It's just the way the 'game' is played and the big question for me, as I said, is whether I have the courage to speed down this "lane" and allow myself to die.

And die should be in quotes, because as I said, there's the definite knowledge that I will continue in some other form, as in reincarnation. This is the end of Bruce but it leads to continuation in another form, or another body.

So I'm with some friends whom I do not at this moment know who they were and it seems like there's only a couple of people present with me. And I don't any more about who they are.

Let me see if I can describe this succinctly.

A bowling lane type arrangement in which we choose to propel ourselves or be propelled down this lane-like space, roughly the length of a bowling alley. We propel ourselves or are propelled towards this opening in a wall like a hole and then a tunnel in the wall in which something like a spinning blade or a vertically arranged garbage disposal ends our life.

But it's like the tunnel somehow continues on past that, though I'm not sure what happens . . . it's like our life is ended right near the beginning of this "tunnel" but then the "tunnel" continues beyond that and . . . not aware of what it's like afterwards.

And can I get up the courage to do this? Can I get up the courage to end my life in this way, knowing that it's painless, my life will continue in another form as in reincarnation.

As I wake up the question is, maybe the reason I'm too scared to do this, or reluctant to do this, is that I haven't said goodbye. Since this is gonna be the end of Bruce, maybe if I say goodbye to people I will then have the courage to do this, as my friends seem to have the courage to do this.

So for a variety of reasons this is unlike any dream I've had. I haven't recorded any dreams in months at least. This is such an interesting dream and there seems like such a strong spiritual truth in this dream. The basic premise seems to contain so much in it that relates to reality as I know it. One of those truths being the fact that this life is game-like as I understand it, and that we do reincarnate, and that courage *is* required.

What's different is that we don't usually decide to end our lives so definitively and so consciously. And of course, the physical means of ending life here is not like anything I know.

Suicide doesn't seem like the word to use for this dream because suicide immediately carries the notion of despair. In this dream there wasn't the slightest sense of despair. It was not ending life because of a feeling of hopelessness or powerlessness but it was ending life because that's how the game is played.

This 'bowling-lane-like' space that you speed down, if anything it's shorter than a bowling lane, not longer than it. And to each side of this "lane" there's nothing whatsoever like another lane so I don't have a clear idea or image of the space within which this "lane" exists.

Maybe the name for this dream would be the 'bowling lane' of conscious, intentional, embodiment termination, because death is not accurate here since reincarnation is understood, so life termination seems somehow more appropriate, since you are choosing to end one embodiment to set the stage for another.

The 'bowling lane' of conscious, intentional, embodiment termination."

(This is the Appendix to *Bowling and Reincarnation* in Chapter 17. Move on now to Chapter 18.)

Works Cited

Anonymous. (2015). Retrieved 2015, from Yahoo Answers: https://answers.yahoo.com/question/index?qid=20141210144926AADoV0w

Bailey, Jake (2014. September 7). Retrieved September 7, 2014, from Skeptiko Forum. http://www.skeptiko-forum.com/

Dicus, J. (n.d.). Retrieved February 11, 2017, from www.near-death.com: http://www.near-death.com/reincarnation/experiences/jeanie-dicus.html. First published in P.M.H. Atwater's book, "Beyond the Light" (1994)

Dossey, L. (2009). *The Power of Premonitions.*

Dunne, J. W. *An Experiment With Time.*

Hoberman, J. (2015, August 26). Retrieved August 26, 2015, from www.nytimes.com: https://www.nytimes.com/2015/08/30/movies/the-tall-blond-man-with-one-black-shoe-cloak-and-dagger-and-farce.html?_r=0

Kennedy, Jim E. (2014, February 12). Retrieved February 12, 2014 from Michael Prescott's Blog: http://michaelprescott.typepad.com/michael_prescotts_blog/2014/02/a-mess.html

Kovalinsky, S. (2008, September 5). Retrieved February 25, 2016, from Anthony Peake: http://www.anthonypeake.com/forum/viewtopic.php?f=8&t=145

Maury, A. (1865). *Sleep and Dreams.* Paris: Didier.

Prescott, M. (2015, November 15). Retrieved 2015, from Michael Prescott's Blog: http://michaelprescott.typepad.com/michael_prescotts_blog/2015/11/skepticism-on-the-couch.html

Setmayer, T. (2015). Retrieved August 7, 2015, from CNN.com.

Taverner, J. (2008, September 3). Retrieved 2015, from Anthony Peake: http://www.anthonypeake.co.uk/forum/viewtopic.php?f=12&t=152

To Access *The Evidence at a Glance*

Go to: http://brucesiegel.net/book/

Use the password: EAAGu&gKL1h9*sX

About The Author

Bruce Siegel lives, writes, and dreams in Southern California, where he is also known as a pianist and music educator. His passion is exploring the larger meaning of psychic ability—what it says about who and what we really are. Follow his blog at BruceSiegel.net; contact him at Bruce@BruceSiegel.net.

www.ingramcontent.com/pod-product-compliance
Lightning Source LLC
LaVergne TN
LVHW061257060426
835508LV00015B/1399